Northern Asia

MANAGING EDITORS
Amy Bauman
Barbara J. Behm

CONTENT EDITORS
Amanda Barrickman
James I. Clark
Patricia Lantier
Charles P. Milne, Jr.
Katherine C. Noonan
Christine Snyder
Gary Turbak
William M. Vogt
Denise A. Wenger
Harold L. Willis
John Wolf

ASSISTANT EDITORS
Ann Angel
Michelle Dambeck
Barbara Murray
Renee Prink
Andrea J. Schneider

INDEXER
James I. Clark

ART/PRODUCTION
Suzanne Beck, Art Director
Andrew Rupniewski, Production Manager
Eileen Rickey, Typesetter

Library of Congress Number: 88-18337

2 3 4 5 6 7 8 9 0   97 96 95 94 93 92

Library of Congress Cataloging-in-Publication Data

Burton, Fiona Grace, 1958-
  [Asia settentrionale. English]
  Northern Asia / Fiona Grace Burton, Robert Lea.

  — (World nature encyclopedia)
  Translation of: Asia settentrionale.
  Includes index.
  Summary: Discusses the natural and ecological niches,
boundaries, and plant and animal life of Asia's wildlife
habitats.
  1. Ecology—Asia—Juvenile literature. [1. Ecology—
Asia.] I. Lea, Robert, 1956-. II. Title. III. Series. IV. Series:
Natural nel mondo. English.
  QH179.B8713 1988 574.5'264'095—dc19   88-18330
  ISBN 0-8172-3325-3

WORLD NATURE ENCYCLOPEDIA

Northern Asia

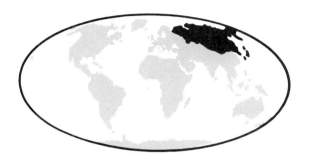

Fiona Grace Burton
Robert Lea

RAINTREE
STECK-VAUGHN
L I B R A R Y

Austin, Texas

CONTENTS

INTRODUCTION

Northern Asia is a vast and extremely varied region. It takes in Tibet, Mongolia, the Himalayas, Siberia, and the Ural Mountains, Japan, and China.

China is located in the eastern part of the Asian continent. The easternmost coastal part of this country has some of the richest plant and animal populations in the world. Here, in unique environments, one finds unusual plant and animal species. Unfortunately, however, their numbers are constantly declining. Examples are the variegated (marked with different colors) lemur (a type of monkey), the Chinese river dolphin, and the famous giant panda.

Japan lies east of China. It is made up of a long series of volcanic islands. The islands have a long history of great earthquakes and fearsome tidal waves. Like eastern China, Japan has extensive forests of broad-leafed trees.

A large region of plateaus and mountains is also found in northern Asia. The outstanding features of this region are

the Karakoram and Pamir mountains and the Himalayas. The distant and dry plateaus of Tibet and Mongolia are inhabited by numerous species of hoofed animals. These include the Mongolian wild horse and the yak.

To the north is the taiga. This is a great expanse of conifer forests (cone-bearing trees that do not shed their leaves in the fall) lying to the south of the Arctic region. The greatest of these forests is found in Siberia.

Lake Baikal is located at the southern edge of the taiga. This lake is the oldest, largest, and deepest freshwater lake in the world.

South of the taiga is a vast steppe. This is a dry, grass-covered plain with scattered trees and strong winds. The steppe extends westward to the Ural Mountains. Further west of the Urals, the main vegetation is a dense temperate forest.

CHINA: THE EASTERN COASTAL REGION

China is an immense country. It covers an area of about 3.9 million square miles (10 million square kilometers). This is an area greater than the entire surface of the United States or western Europe.

With respect to plants and animals, the country can be divided into two halves. This chapter discusses the eastern half, where farms produce over 90 percent of the food needed by the Chinese people.

Climate

During the winter, a large mass of cold air moves eastward from the interior regions of Asia. This is called the winter monsoon, and it brings clear and dry weather. In the summer, masses of ocean air moving westward bring the region abundant rainfall. This air movement is called the summer monsoon. The annual rainfall varies from 18 to 74 inches (500 to 2,000 millimeters), which decreases as one goes north. The annual rainfall is higher in the southeast.

The southern part of the country has a tropical maritime (on or near the sea) climate. The northern part has a cold continental climate. In the summer, the average temperature is above 68° Fahrenheit (20° Celsius) in the entire eastern part of the country. In the winter, however, there is at least a 50°F (28°C) difference in temperature between north and south.

Vegetation

The vegetation of eastern China is extremely rich and varied. There are more than 25,000 plant species. By comparison Europe can boast only 12,000 plant species. Despite centuries of deforestation (the cutting of trees), one can still find examples of all the main types of forest of the world in China. However, many of these forests grow in mountainous regions, because all the level areas are used for farming. To the northeast, the Greater Khingan mountain chain is covered by conifer forests. The dominant trees of these forests are larches, Scotch pines, and Asian birches.

The forests of the Lesser Khingan Mountains are known for their Korean pines and Dahurian larches. Proceeding southward toward the Yangtze River, there are more mixed forests of oaks, maples, lime trees, Korean pines, and Manchurian walnuts. South of the Yangtze, there are subtropical evergreen forests composed of various species of magnolias, tea trees, and laurels. The camphor tree and bamboo are also common. In the valleys and along the

Preceding pages: The taiga is the northernmost forest of the Eurasian continent. It is formed by conifer forests. These forests occupy a large part of the cold lands of northeastern Asia. They also cover the neighboring regions of northern Europe. Beyond the taiga lies the tundra. The frozen soils of the tundra allow only the growth of low, scrub vegetation.

Opposite page: The lesser panda, along with the giant panda, is one of the most interesting and well-known inhabitants of the Asian mountains. The lesser panda lives at higher elevations than the giant panda. It also has a wider distribution. This animal is found from Nepal to the eastern Himalaya Mountains and in southwestern China.

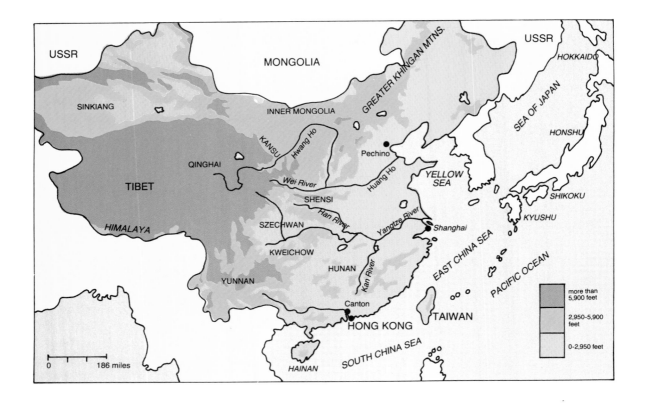

This map of China shows the elevation, main rivers, and provinces of the eastern coastal region.

coasts, there are large orchards of orange, banana, and litchi trees. In the far southern part, one finds tropical forests.

Unfortunately, over the course of the centuries, vast areas of forest have been cut down. For example, the wood of the Masson pine was highly valued in ancient China. Because so many of these trees have been cut over the years, this species has now become rare. The extensive cutting of the forests has led to a serious problem of soil erosion. The results of erosion became tragically evident in 1981. Because of deforestation in the upper part of the Yangtze River basin, a disastrous flood occurred downstream.

Many different ornamental trees (for decoration) were brought from China to European countries. Among these are the beautiful magnolias, flowering cherries, and various maples. Some of the maples have smooth, orangish trunks. Others have multi-colored bark, which resembles snakeskin.

The southwestern part of China, bordering Burma and Tibet, has perhaps the highest plant concentration of all the temperate climate areas in the world. This area is called the "Sino-Himalayan" region. During the last ice age (up to about twenty thousand years ago), it remained free of ice

Rhododendrons are especially abundant in the mountains of north-central Asia. They are found in southern China and the Himalayas, all the way to Japan. There are about three hundred species of rhododendrons in these regions. Today, many species are used as ornamental shrubs in numerous gardens throughout Europe and the United States. The photograph shows a rhododendron in the Wolong Nature Reserve in China.

and the plants were not killed. Thus, the plants kept many genetic traits from which many groups of species evolved. From 80 to 90 percent of all the known species of primroses and rhododendrons are found here. This region is considered a paradise for plant collectors.

A typical mountain slope in Yunnan Province, between elevations of 6,560 and 9,840 feet (2,000 and 3,000 meters), is covered by a multicolored band of a mixed broadleaf forest. This forest is composed of Chinese species of alder, mountain ash, polar, maple, willow, cherry, birch, and hazelnut. Also included are such bushes as butterfly-bushes, blueberries, and barberries. Rhododendron shrubs are abundant, with flowers ranging in color from deep red to yellow.

Above 9,840 feet (3,000 m), conifer trees as well as thickets of rhododendrons and bamboo are found. There are numerous Yunnan pines and Armand's pines. Armand's pine was named after the French explorer, Armand David.

At higher elevations are the Delavay fir and Tibetan larch. The forest clearings are covered by anemones, lilies, and delphiniums. Still higher, one finds alpine meadows and enormous amounts of rock fragments. Many species of gentians, primroses, and dwarf rhododendrons grow here.

The big-headed turtle lives in the mountain streams of southern China. It reaches a length of 5.5 inches (14 cm), with an equally long tail. The female lays two eggs at a time. The eggs are laid in a hole dug in the ground along the riverbank.

Animals

In ancient times, rhinoceroses, saber-toothed tigers, wolves, and stegodons (extinct, primitive elephants) lived in the northern forests. Deer, gazelles, and ostriches lived on the plains of the steppe. Changes in climate led to the disappearance of a large number of these animals. Nevertheless, animals are not scarce today in China. It has been estimated that at least four hundred species of mammals are present in this country, as well as more than 1,100 bird species.

Reptiles

The majority of reptiles in china are tropical species that live in the southern part of the country.

The extraordinary big-headed turtle lives in mountain streams. Its head is armored with thick, horny plates. Another unusual reptile group consists of the soft-shelled turtles. The Chinese three-clawed turtle is probably the most interesting species of this group. Instead of having a shell of horny plates, these turtles have a leathery skin.

The Malayan monitor is one of the four monitor species inhabiting the Asian continent. Unlike the other three, the Malayan monitor has aquatic habits. It can swim across wide arms of the sea. At the southern area of its distribution, it has reached the island of Sri Lanka. The Malayan monitor feeds on fish, crustaceans, and frogs. It has also been known to eat small mammals, birds, eggs, and animal carcasses. It lays from fifteen to thirty eggs. Although it does not reach the size of the gigantic Komodo dragon, its 10-foot (3-m) length makes it one of the largest lizards in the world. (The Komodo dragon is another species of monitor lizard of the Sunda Islands.)

A great majority of the lizards are small. An exception is the massive Chinese water dragon, which can exceed a length of 27 inches (70 centimeters). This reptile has a brilliant olive green color, with dark rings around its crested tail. Another unusual lizard found in southern China is the Indian bloodsucker lizard. During the mating season, its head is a magnificent scarlet red color. The butterfly lizard is even more striking in appearance. Its yellowish orange underside contrasts with beautiful shades of brown and olive green on the back. Another large lizard is the Malayan monitor. This animal is at least 10 feet (3 m) long. It lives in the rain forests and on riverbanks in southern China and on the island of Hainan.

The nonpoisonous snakes include several agile rat snakes. These reptiles prey on small vertebrate animals (animals with a backbone). Another example of nonpoisonous snake is the fishing water snake. It waits for its prey by remaining motionless in the water, with the tip of its nose above the surface. Its diet consists mainly of fish and frogs.

The pit vipers are the most evolved snakes. They kill their victims with poison. These animals are characterized by a pit on each side of the head, between the nostril and the eye. The two pits are sense organs. They enable the pit vipers to detect slight differences in temperature. They are able to precisely locate warm-blooded prey by the heat given off by its body. One of the snakes in this group is the Chinese copperhead.

The long fangs of pit vipers are folded to the rear of the mouth when not in use. When used, the fangs straighten out from their folded position. The fangs of the Chinese habu, another pit viper, are 0.5 inch (15 mm) long. Many people have died from its poisonous bite.

The majority of pit vipers protect their eggs by keeping them within the body until ready to hatch. Consequently, they give birth to live young. The mountain pit viper lays its eggs, however. The eggs are attentively watched by the mother until they hatch.

There are only two species of alligators in the world. The more familiar species lives in the southern part of North America. The other species is smaller, measuring about 6.5 feet (2 m) long. It is found only in China, along the hidden bends of the Yangtze River basin. In these areas, it moves among the reeds and bushes. Unfortunately, this species has suffered a great reduction in number, due to extensive hunting by humans. The meat of the Chinese alligator is consi-

The Chinese alligator is closely related to the American alligator. It became known to scientists of the Western countries in only 1879. However, Marco Polo had already described this animal many centuries before. The Chinese alligator feeds on various aquatic animals, from fish to marsh snails. It is especially fond of turtles. The female lays the eggs along the banks of rivers and streams, within a nest made from marsh grasses. She watches over the nest until the eggs hatch. To save this species from extinction, the Chinese government has established several nature reserves. In the reserves, this alligator is raised and studied.

dered a choice food. Today, the Chinese alligator is being studied at several research centers. Researchers have succeeded in artificially incubating (keeping warm) the alligator's eggs until they hatch.

Birds

The birds in China belong to more than 1,100 different species. This is equal to 14 percent of the total bird species in the world. The majority of the species are found in the eastern half of the country.

In the cold northeastern part there are numerous

mountain francolins (a type of partridge), common pheasants, and Dahurian partridges. Birds common to the Northern Hemisphere, such as rock ptarmigans and snow finches, nest in these regions. Other birds of the Northern Hemisphere spend the winter here. These include the snow buntings and the snowy owls. Typical birds of open zones are found in the areas that are intensively farmed. Some of these birds are the buntings, larks, wagtails, egrets, and herons. The tropical plains and hills of the south and the island of Hainan are home to numerous exotic (unusual) birds. These include peacock pheasants, fruit pigeons, sunbirds, and flowerpeckers.

The central lowlands of the Yangtze River basin are dotted with lakes. The lakes are ideal for the wintering of a large variety of aquatic birds. Parrots, scarlet finches, eared pheasants, and babbling thrushes inhabit the forests of southwestern China.

The pheasants live in almost any type of environment, except deserts. This group of birds originated in Asia. More than eighteen species of pheasants are native to China.

The short-tailed pheasants are rather stout, with short, square tails. The back of the males is either green, blue, or violet, with a metallic (metal-like) tint. Their underside is of a shiny black color. The females are brown, with markings of different colors (variegated). The short-tailed pheasants use their strong beaks to dig in the soil in search of bulbs and plant roots.

The eared pheasants also live in mountainous zones. The males and females have the same plumage. The plumage is thick, with a long tail and long white feathers at the sides of the head (hence the name "eared pheasants"). These birds have patches of skin on the head, called "wattles." The brown eared pheasant has now become rare in the wild, due to extensive hunting.

The blue eared pheasant is also close to extinction in China, its country of origin. For centuries, high-ranking government officials in China used the feathers of this species to decorate their hats. This led to a great demand for these feathers.

Two beautiful birds of the same genus are the golden pheasant and the Lady Amherst pheasant. The mating dance of the golden pheasant is an impressive sight. The male, with the feathers of the crest and the collar erect, jumps around the female, making high-pitched sounds.

The herons and egrets are characterized by long legs

15

and necks and long, slender beaks. They are usually found in rice paddies and on the banks of canals and rivers, where they hunt for fish and frogs. Several species, such as the gray heron and the cattle egret, are found in many places. They have spread beyond the continent. Other species are found only in China. These include the rare white-eared night heron of Hainan Island, and the more common Chinese pond heron. This last heron nests in many places in China. Another exclusive species is the rare Chinese white egret. It nests in southern China, but winters much further south, in Indonesia and the Philippine Islands.

The minivets are insect-eating birds, typical of southern and eastern Asia. The orange minivet is 8 inches (20 cm) long. The male has a black plumage with a reddish orange underside and lower back. Its throat is also black. The

The mandarin duck originated in China and Japan. In the past, it was not found in Europe nor in America. By now, however, it has been imported into these two continents, where it reproduces successfully in several regions. It is often seen in ponds, marshes, and small lakes. In the Oriental tradition, a wedding gift of a pair of mandarin ducks symbolizes fidelity.

female has a brilliant black-and-yellow color throughout. The mountain minivet and the long-tailed minivet have similar coloring. The ashy minivet, however, has duller colors. The minivets live among the tree foliage (leaves). These beautiful birds are interesting to observe as large flocks in the trees call out to other flocks before gathering.

Often one finds babbling thrushes alongside minivets. The babbling thrushes compose a large family of birds of various shapes and colors. About thirty species of this family are found only in China or in nearby regions. The babbling thrushes are not skilled flyers. They live mainly in the underbrush of the forest, and feed mainly on insects. Outside of the mating season, they often move about in flocks, going here and there in search of food. The scimitar babbler has a long, curved beak and a medium-sized tail.

The Chinese river dolphin is found in Lake Tungting and the nearby sections of the Yangtze River. For a long time, the local people worshipped this animal, believing that it had once been a princess who had been swallowed up by the water. The animal resembles the dolphins living in other river systems of India and South America. It is characterized by a small size, a long slender snout, small eyes, small rounded fins, and numerous teeth. The fishermen of the Hunan Province believe that anyone who harms these dolphins will be cursed by bad luck. Just the same, until the species became protected by law in 1975, dolphins were captured along the course of the Yangtze River. The local people once used some parts of this animal to produce medicines.

The laughing thrush has a short beak and tail.

The scaly-breasted laughing thrush is about 4 inches (10 cm) long. Its tail is so short that it is hardly visible. The melodious laughing thrushes are medium-sized birds. They are generally brown in color.

The splendidly colored sunbirds also live in southern China. Their diet consists almost entirely of nectar, and they are often seen hopping among the flowering branches of trees. The sunbirds inhabit many environments, including dry heaths (open waterlands), gardens and forests. Their nests are large sack-shaped structures that seem to hang unsteadily from the tree branches. The sunbirds of the *Aetophyga* genus are small and very attractive. The magnificent plumage of the males is a metallic green or blue violet with scattered feathers that are blood red or brilliant yellow.

The barbets nest mostly in holes and cavities, and they are usually found in forests and thickets. However, they are also seen in cities, where they are attracted by fruit trees. The Asian species of barbets are generally green, with red or yellow heads. They are characterized by thick, silky tufts of feathers at the base of the beak. The barbets also are known for their monotonous calls. In some species, such as the great Himalayan barbet, the male and female sing duets. Once every second the male makes a sad "pi-u-u" sound to which the female responds once every four seconds.

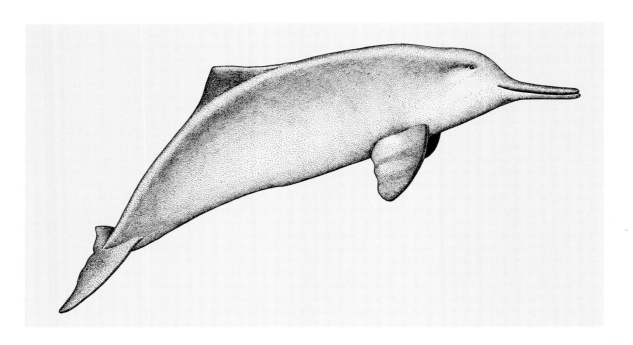

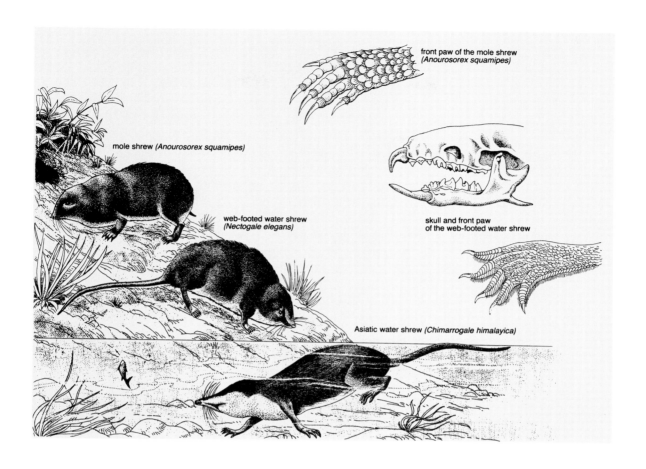

front paw of the mole shrew
(*Anourosorex squamipes*)

mole shrew (*Anourosorex squamipes*)

web-footed water shrew
(*Nectogale elegans*)

skull and front paw
of the web-footed water shrew

Asiatic water shrew (*Chimarrogale himalayica*)

The remote mountains of Szechwan Province are inhabited by various species of insect-eating mammals. Some live under the ground in burrows, while others inhabit bodies of water. The mole shrew is found from the Szechwan to the Tonkin region. It has long claws for digging tunnels. The web-footed water shrew is found only along the streams of the southeastern Himalaya region. In this region, it hunts small fish. The Asiatic water shrew is also an able fisher. When it swims under the water, it is able to seal its ears completely with skin flaps. Shrews communicate with each other by high-pitched chirping sounds. It is believed that the sounds may also serve as a sonar device.

Insect-eating Mammals

Many species of insect-eating mammals live in the eastern part of China. One of these is the spiny hedgehog, which is found throughout Asia and Europe. The moon rats are less well known. They are similar to mice and are found in Southeast Asia. The shrews are micelike animals that are widespread. Most of the species live on land, although several shrews live near water and are aquatic. An example is the webfooted water shrew, which inhabits the mountain forests of the central and southern regions.

The Asiatic shrew mole is related to the shrews, which it resembles in appearance. It is found in southwestern China. The majority of the mole species have cylindrical bodies, very small eyes, and sensitive noses. They are characterized by strong paws that are adapted to burrowing in the ground while searching for prey. The Kansu mole is rarely seen. Only a few specimens have been collected and preserved in museums.

The variegated langur inhabits bamboo forests in the high mountains of the Szechwan, Kansu, and Yunnan provinces. It is identified by a golden belly and a blackish brown back, with patches of long silver hair. The top part of the snout is a bluish color.

Rodents

Many species of mice, rats, voles (mouselike animals with short tails), squirrels, and flying squirrels are widespread throughout China. Typical rodents of eastern China include the rock squirrels. Some zoologists think these animals are the link between the chipmunks and the true squirrels. The mole rats are stocky animals that resemble moles. They are about 8 inches (20 cm) long, with a thick silky fur and strong paws that are used for digging. These animals are widely hunted in China because of the damage they cause to farm crops.

The Père David's vole is about half the size of the mole rat. It has a reddish brown color and lives at high elevations. A similar species is the red-backed vole. This rodent causes great damages to the pine forests because it eats the seeds of the Korean pine. Therefore, it prevents the spreading of this tree species. The Chinese jumping mouse receives its name from its long hind legs and its running and climbing abilities. It lives in the cooler forests near rivers and streams. Its nests are built on the ground, and have characteristic circular shapes.

Monkeys

The most numerous and adaptable monkeys of Asia are the macaques, which are represented by many species in southern China. One of these is the rhesus macaque, which has a brown coat with reddish tinted hind parts. It is 2 feet (60 cm) tall, with a 12-inch (30-cm) tail.

The Assam macaque is a large monkey with a thick fur. It inhabits areas that are higher in elevation than those normally occupied by the rhesus macaque.

Another group of macaques is characterized by short tails or lack tails entirely. Particularly interesting among this group is the cropped-tail macaque of southeastern China. This monkey has a snout of a brilliant red color that is sometimes spotted with blue.

The Tibetan macaque is another macaque found in China. This large, hairy monkey has a brown bearded face. All the macaques live in large social groups. They spend most of their time on the ground, although their limbs and eyes are adapted to a life in the trees. The macaques have complex brains and a great learning capacity.

In China, the macaques and langurs (a genus of slender, long-tailed monkeys) inhabit the same areas. However, the two groups of monkeys seldom compete with each other for

The rhesus macaque is found over a large area from northern Pakistan to southern China and Southeast Asia. This forest animal lives in groups. Research conducted on the blood of the rhesus macaque has led to the discovery of the so-called Rh factor.

Following pages: A giant panda eats in a bamboo thicket in the Wolong Nature Reserve in the Province of Szechwan. This animal is among the rarest mammals on earth. It has inhabited China for at least 600,000 years. It has been known to the Western countries only since 1869, when the French missionary priest Père Armand David saw it for the first time.

food. The macaques are omnivores, meaning they eat both animals and plants. The langurs feed on leaves.

Most of the species of langurs have brilliant colors. Some species, such as the variegated langur, have peculiar noses, pointing upward. A similar species, Brelich's langur, is found in the Kweichow Province. Both the variegated and the Brelich's langurs are rare today. Little is known about their habits. As far back as the year 2000 B.C., the ancient Chinese used animal figures that strongly resemble these monkeys to decorate their vases.

Pandas

The giant panda is the symbol of the World Wildlife Fund. Although it is rare, much is known about this mammal. It is considered to be related to the bears, with which it has a general resemblance. This animal differs from the

21

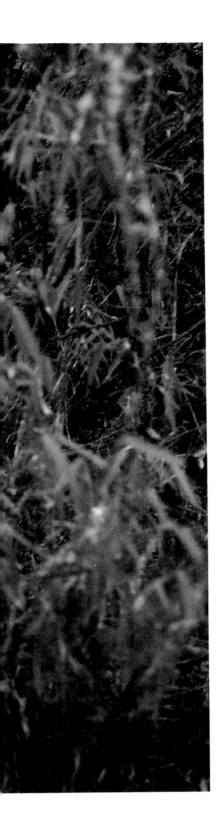

bear in its unusual coloring, a longer wrist bone that functions as a thumb, and certain aspects of its diet. The giant panda's diet consists almost entirely of bamboo shoots. This animal can easily chew the shoots with the help of large, flat molars. Although bamboo is available year-round, it has a low nutrient value. The giant panda does not have the necessary bacteria in its intestines to efficiently digest the bamboo. Therefore, an adult giant panda must spend at least ten to twelve hours a day gathering and eating 33 to 44 pounds (15 to 20 kilograms) of bamboo in order to survive.

Bamboo plants usually reproduce by the growth of new plants from an already existing plant. This is called vegetative reproduction, as opposed to reproducing by flowering and seed formations. Bamboo plants flower and produce seeds only once, after a long period of growth. Several species produce flowers only after forty years of growth. The bamboo plants die soon after flowering. Between 1974 and 1976, in the Min Mountains, several species of bamboo plants suddenly flowered and then died. This caused the death of more than one hundred pandas by starvation.

In prehistoric times, the panda inhabited most of eastern China. However, extensive hunting and the destruction of its habitat led to the disappearance of this animal from a large part of its original area. Today, it survives in several dense mixed forests of bamboo and conifers where the climate is particularly cold and humid. The panda is found only in six small areas along the eastern edge of the Tibetan plateau. These include the provinces of Szechwan, Kansu, and Shensi at elevations between 3,900 and 11,100 feet (1,200 and 3,400 m). A population count taken in the mid-1970s indicated that only about a thousand pandas survived in the wild.

The first steps to protect this species were taken in 1957. There are presently twelve reserves for the protection of the panda. They cover a total area of 2,316 square miles (6,000 sq. km). In 1980, the Wolong Nature Reserve, with the assistance of the World Wildlife Fund and the Chinese government, began a research program for the study of the panda in the wild. The program was coordinated by Hu Jinchu and George Schaller.

Pandas normally live alone, and are territorial animals. They mark their territories by using scent markings. The average life span of pandas is from twenty to thirty years. These animals do not mate before the age of six or seven years. Though they successfully reproduce in the wild, they do not succeed as well in captivity, because the conditions for their breeding are hard to recreate.

The lesser panda has a certain resemblance to the giant panda. It is, however, an entirely different animal. It is somewhat similar to a cat and has beautiful colors. Its body is covered by a thick, reddish fur, while its snout is white with dark stripes. The tail is bushy and ringed. During the day, it sleeps curled up like a cat. It feeds at night, eating bamboo, fruits, and roots.

Wild Cats

The tiger originated in Siberia during the ice age, about fifty thousand years ago. From Siberia, it gradually migrated south. There are now several varieties of the tiger species according to location. The Siberian tiger is found in northwestern China. The Chinese variety of tiger is found in eastern China, and the Indonesian variety is scattered in various areas of southern China. Only about one hundred tigers of the Chinese variety now exist.

At one time, leopards were also widespread throughout China and most of Asia. However, their populations have since greatly decreased or disappeared altogether. This is due to the growing demand for their beautiful furs. The small clouded leopard is still found in the mountain forests of southwestern China and Taiwan. It has a striped yellowish brown coat with black spots.

The leopard cat belongs to a group of smaller cats. These animals are especially numerous in Southeast Asia. The leopard cat is about 2 feet (60 cm) long and has a spotted coat. The leopard cats in central and southern China have coats that vary in color from olive yellow to brown. The leopard cats of northern China, Mongolia, and the Himalayas are yellowish gray or silver gray. This difference in coloring follows the so-called Gloger's rule. According to this rule, animals in warm, humid climates are darker in color than their relatives of the colder regions. In northern China, the leopard cats give birth to two to four young in May. In the southern part of their distribution area, the young are born throughout the year.

Deer

Fossil evidence indicates that the evolution of the deer family originally took place in Asia. The evidence also suggests that the most primitive ancestors of the group

Opposite page: A considerable number of deer species evolved in eastern Asia. The drawing and picture show three of the species inhabiting this region. The Chinese water deer lacks antlers but has unusually long canine teeth that extend out of the mouth. The Chinese muntjac has short antlers that are supported by a bony stem. The musk deer *(in the photograph)* also lacks antlers and has very long upper canine teeth. The male has a characteristic sack on the underside that gives off a strong musk odor. This musk fluid is used to make perfumes.

Chinese water deer

Chinese muntjac deer

lacked horns. They resembled present species of deer such as the small musk deer and the Chinese water deer. Both of these species measure about 22 inches (55 cm) at the shoulder.

The musk deer are shy and solitary animals. They inhabit forests and steppes between elevations of 9,800 and 13,100 feet (3,000 and 4,000 m) in the Chinese, Siberian, and Himalayan regions. The males have large canine (pointed, tearing) teeth that are similar to tusks. They also have a musk gland that produces a brown, waxy musk fluid with a strong odor. This scent is used to mark the males' territories. The musk fluid has long been used for producing medicines and perfumes. At most, only one ounce of musk can be extracted from one gland. The hunting of the musk deer for commercial purposes nearly led to the extinction of this animal in several zones. Nevertheless, the musk deer is being successfully raised in captivity in southern China.

The Chinese water deer is found in the basin of the Yangtze River and in Korea. It lives in small family groups among the reeds and tall grasses of riverbanks and in cultivated fields. The males have tusks and, like the musk deer,

use them as weapons in fights with rival males. These fights take place during the rutting season (time of sexual excitement), when the male wishes to win rights to a female for mating.

The muntjac deer of Southeast Asia are more evolved than the last two deer species mentioned. They have tusks as well as simple antlers. The Chinese muntjac, the hairy-fronted muntjac, and the Tibetan muntjac inhabit the edge of the forests or thick vegetation. They are found mainly on the slopes of hills in eastern and southern China.

Millions of years ago, a primitive deer resembling the muntjacs gave rise to the large-sized deer with impressive antlers. These large deer include the common Eurasian

Two male Pere David's deer fight in the Duke of Bedford Park in Woburn Abbey, England. English zoologists hope to send a number of these animals to China to establish a wild population in the original area of the species (it is now extinct in China). The deer are to be taken from zoos in Chester, Whipsnade, and Marwell, in England.

deer, the sika deer, and the Père David's deer. The sika deer is a close relative of the common deer. It is about 4 feet (1.2 m) tall at the shoulder, with a stout body and a spotted coat. The antlers are modest in size. The tail of the sika deer is completely white.

The Père David's deer is now extinct in its original environments, which are the marshy plains of northeastern China. It disappeared from this region about 1,800 years ago. However, a herd of these deer survived in the Imperial Hunting Park in Beijing, China. It was here that the famous missionary priest and and naturalist Père Armand David discovered it. Animals in captivity that have descended from this herd are now found in many parts of the world.

The takin is a sturdy animal, which is distantly related to the chamois. It lives in the regions of Assam, Nepal, and Bhutan, and in the Chinese provinces of Szechwan and Shensi. It prefers forest environments and thickets at high elevations, even up to 13,000 feet (4,000 m). The males live alone, except during the mating season, from July to August. After a pregnancy of eight months, the female gives birth to one offspring. At only three days of life, the young takin is able to follow the mother while grazing.

The most famous herd is found in the park of the estate of the Duke of Bedford in Woburn Abbey, England. Unfortunately, the herd that lived in the Imperial Hunting Park in Beijing was largely wiped out by a flood in 1894, and by later hunts. The Père David's deer has unusual antlers, a long tail, and large, spreading hooves.

Mountain Goats

The takin, the Sumatran serow, and the goral live in the mountainous territories of eastern Asia. They belong to a primitive group of animals that are found only in remote areas. Their limited areas of distribution result from the strong competition with more aggressive species of wild goats and sheep.

The takin is a wild goat that is found only in central and southwestern China. It inhabits steep mountain slopes above 7,900 feet (2,400 m) of elevation. It frequents thickly wooded areas, especially jungles of bamboo and rhododendrons. This animal makes narrow, regular trails in the underbrush. During the summer season, it migrates in herds above the tree limit to feed in the high mountain zone of dwarf shrubs. The takin has a strong, stout body with a thick

coat of hair. It measures a little over 3 feet (1 m) at the shoulder. Its snout resembles that of a domestic goat. The takin of the Szechwan Province has a yellow coat during the summer and a gray coat in the winter. The takin of the Shensi Province is mainly whitish yellow or golden in color. In ancient times, the native people hunted these animals for their meat. Today, however, they are protected by law.

The Sumatran serow and the goral are similar in appearance. They both have stout bodies and resemble goats. They inhabit harsh mountainous regions that are covered by forests. The gorals are identified by their smaller size, which never exceeds 38 inches (1 m) in height. They have shorter horns and generally prefer higher elevations and more rugged terrain than the Sumatran serows. The gorals usually live in small herds. The Sumatran serows, however, are solitary animals. Both species feed and are more active in the early morning and at dusk. They are often hunted for sport, and they are preyed upon by leopards. Birds of prey attack their young.

The goral vaguely resembles a goat and is associated with rocky regions. It normally prefers high elevations, but it has also been found near the sea. Its diet varies with the season. It eats plants in the summer, tree leaves and buds in the fall, and twigs and acorns in the winter. The female goral gives birth to one or two young after a pregnancy of about six months.

JAPAN

Japan is composed of a group of islands. The four largest islands are Hokkaido, Honshu, Shikoku, and Kyushu. In addition, more than three thousand smaller islands make up this country. The island group extends from north to south over a distance of 1,488 miles (2,400 km). The islands are located in the heart of a north-south belt that is characterized by frequent earthquake activity. The islands have been formed in relatively recent times, and are affected by many earthquakes. Mount Fuji is the most spectacular and famous of the islands volcanoes. This volcano became inactive in 1707. Mountain ranges make up about three-fourths of the country, and are covered by dense forests. Many spectacular volcanic lakes, countless hot springs, and steep gorges are found throughout the country.

Climate

Japan is characterized by a wide variety of climates. In the winter months, cold air masses arrive from Siberia, bringing abundant snowfalls. In the summer, a tropical type of climate prevails, influenced by the warm southern currents. Maximum rainfall occurs in the months of June and July. This period is followed by the typhoon season, which lasts from August to October. The average annual rainfall of the country reaches 60 inches (1,600 mm), with a maximum of over 150 inches (4,000 mm) in several zones.

Plants

Thousands of years ago, the islands of Japan were united with the rest of the Asian continent. As a result, the Japanese territory has a large variety of plants in relation to its size. Many of the plants are similar to those of China. Japan was not greatly affected by the glaciers that formed during the ice age. Since the effects of the ice were not strongly felt in this country, many ancient species of plants that disappeared elsewhere were able to survive here.

In the northern areas, the Kurilian Current causes a general lowering in the temperatures. This is especially the case in the northern part of the island of Honshu. In this area, there are many plant species that originated at much more northern latitudes.

Few countries in the world have a higher percentage of forest cover than Japan, about 68 percent. In the central part of Japan, conifer forests predominate on the mountains above 6,560 feet (2,000 m) of elevation. On Hokkaido, the conifer forests also are found at elevations extending to sea

Opposite page: Rice is the main food of most Asian people. Each population has adopted characteristic methods of rice cultivation. These methods are based on the particular terrain of the different regions and on the local water supply. For example, these Japanese rice paddies (the photograph was taken in Shikoku) differ greatly from those of Cambodia or India. Additionally, rice is the source of sake, the national beverage of Japan.

Bamboo forests are widespread on the island of Honshu, the largest of the numerous islands that make up Japan. Bamboo is actually a giant member of the grass family. It is difficult for any other plants to grow in the shade of these unique forests.

level. The main species of trees are Hondo and Sakhalin spruces.

Sometimes these trees are mixed with Marie's fir and Veitch's fir. Other trees are the Hinoki cypress, the Japanese larch, and the Erman birch, which add variety to the mixed forests. Steep riverbanks are always covered by poplars and willows. In the northern part of Honshu and the southern part of Hokkaido, one finds lush forests of deciduous broad-leaf trees. (Deciduous trees lose their leaves seasonally.) At

higher elevations, these forests are dominated by the crenate beech. A similar species, the Japanese beech, is more common in the lower and warmer zones.

The Japanese cedar and the hiba tree, which resemble a cypress, are impressive species of the Japanese forests. They represent the most important lumber trees for the construction industries of Japan. The stupendous Japanese cedars have a reddish bark and long, slender trunks that reach heights of over 164 feet (50 m). At these heights, they rival the sequoias of California. The Japanese cedars have long life spans. Several trees have been estimated to be over a thousand years old. Some of these ancient cedars have been declared national monuments. Since the middle of the sixteenth century, the Japanese cedar and four other species of cedar were selected among the trees to be strictly protected.

The southern part of Japan, in particular the islands of Shikoku and Kyushu, was once covered by a temperate forest of broadleaf evergreen trees. However, since ancient times, most of the area has been used for farming. This gradually led to the change of most forests into rice paddies and fields for crops. Several patches of these ancient, huge forests still remain within the walls of Buddhist and Shinto temples, They also can be admired in several of the smallest and most remote islands. In these forests, the species worthy of mention are the camphor tree, the evergreen oaks, various podocarpus trees, and pink-flowered albizzia trees. The camphor tree has evergreen leaves. Its trunk contains aromatic oils. These species represent only a small part of the tree species that were once abundant in these ancient forests.

Mangrove forests border the southern coasts of the islands of Ryukyu, while dense thickets of wild fig, palms, and screw pines grow in the interior areas.

It is amazing to consider that a good 35 percent of the sizable area covered by forest has an artificial origin. The main species that can be observed on these tree plantations are Japanese cedar, hinoki cypress, Japanese red pine, and black pine. In the broadleaf plantations, two species of oak (*Quercus glanduliflora* and *Q. acutissima*) and a chestnut species (*Castanopis cuspidata*) are commonly planted.

In 1868, Japan was opened to foreigners who had not been welcomed for more than two hundred years. From that time on, many ornamental Japanese trees were exported, to be planted in many European and American gardens and

For botanists, the region of China and Japan is perhaps the most interesting of all the temperate lands in the Northern Hemisphere. It has an extraordinary variety of plant species. There are at least three hundred genera of plants that are not found anywhere else in the world. These plants are called "endemic," or native, plants. Many of the nonnative plants are related to the plants of neighboring regions. A large number of plants cultivated in Europe and North America originated here. They include both fruit and ornamental plants. The Japanese have had a major role in developing countless varieties of plants over the centuries from wild plant "ancestors." The Japanese maple has been extensively developed into many ornamental varieties. The photograph shows a grape-leaved variety.

parks. These ornamental species were the result of patient genetic crosses developed over the centuries. The trees from which the ornamental trees originally came are by now forgotten.

The Japanese maple is another familiar ornamental species. Through the centuries, more than two hundred varieties were produced from this tree. Each variety differs in the shape of the leaves and in color.

Other Japanese plants present in gardens with many varieties are the bushy Japanese cedars. Over the years, the cedars that kept their young, feathery foliage into advanced age were selected for reproduction. Other plants that were selected over a period of time were several slow-growing varieties of sawara cypresses. Their marvelous shades of color range from green to blue and gold.

Animals

The animals of Japan, like the plants, are characterized by a surprising variety of species. Since Japan was not much affected by glaciers during the ice age, several ancient animal species survived there. An example is the Japanese giant salamander. The north-south location of the Japanese islands results in regions with much different climates. The different climates help produce a large variety of animals.

The zoolgists Watase and Blakiston have identified two lines separating the distribution areas of numerous animal species. The animals that live south of the "Watase Line" have strong links with the animals of the tropical zones of Southeast Asia. For other species, the "Blakiston Line" represents the northern limit of their distribution. The animals of the northern Japanese island of Hokkaido are similar to those of Siberia. They include the mountain hare, the Asiatic chipmunk, the northern pika, and the brown bear. The animals that inhabit the zone between these two biogeographic lines (the distribution of plants and animals according to geography) are generally similar to the animals of northeastern China. These animals include the Japanese macaque, the Asiatic black bear, the Japanese dormouse, and a wide variety of birds. Among the most common birds are the ring-necked pheasant and the Japanese green woodpecker.

The marine animals of Japan include a variety of very beautiful species. These marine animals are particularly

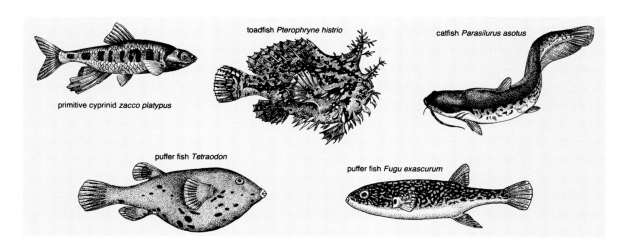

primitive cyprinid *zacco platypus*

toadfish *Pterophryne histrio*

catfish *Parasilurus asotus*

puffer fish *Tetraodon*

puffer fish *Fugu exascurum*

white-headed crane

green sandpiper

Naumann's thrush

tufted puffin

short-tailed albatross

numerous along the coasts of the southernmost islands, which are bordered by coral reefs. There are also small but very poisonous sea snakes. These snakes are found only in the mild coastal waters of the Pacific and Indian oceans. The squids are valued as food by the Japanese people. Fishermen capture them at dawn and at dusk, attracting them with lights. The Japanese spider crab lives along the coasts. It is the largest crustacean inhabiting the waters that surround Japan.

Birds

There are more than four hundred species of birds in Japan. Many of these birds nest elsewhere and migrate to Japan only for the winter. For example, many aquatic birds, such as swans and geese, migrate from Siberia by the thousands to spend the winter in the islands of Honshu and Hokkaido. Huge flocks of white-naped cranes and white-headed cranes fly to southeastern Japan, especially in Arasaki. They migrate from eastern Asia during the winter.

Many important wintering zones for shorebirds are distributed along the Pacific coast. In these zones, one can find the common lapwing, the black-bellied sandpiper, the green sandpiper, and the common snipe. Many species of seed-eaters winter in Japan, including the Naumann's thrush, the siskin, the woodland bunting, and the brambling.

In the summer, many marine birds nest in numerous colonies on the smaller islands. These include albatrosses, shearwaters, gulls, and guillemots. Bird species of the North Pacific nest on the islands of Yururi and Moyururi, near Hokkaido. One of these is the tufted puffin, which is completely black except for a white face. It has long tufts of feathers above the eyes and a red-and-green beak. Another year-round species is the open-water cormorant, a large bark bird with a large tail. It builds its nest with aquatic vegetation and nests on narrow tongues of land, as does the shag cormorant.

The albatrosses are the largest of the flying birds, with a wingspan of over 10 feet (3 m). They are wonderfully adapted to long flights over the open sea. In the past, the short-tailed albatross was widely hunted for its beautiful feathers.

Many species of herons and egrets nest in colonies. In Japan, snowy egrets, great egrets, cattle egrets, night herons, and gray herons are found. They do not often nest on the small islands, however. Many different species sometimes

Japanese crested ibis

Siberian thrush ♂

reed bunting ♂

pine grosbeak ♀

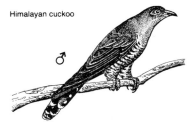

Himalayan cuckoo ♂

nest together in the same rookery, or nesting location. Each species builds its nest at different heights in the same tree. There are several reasons why these birds, as well as others, nest in colonies. First, the colony functions as an "information center," from which the members are informed of areas with abundant food. Another reason is greater protection from the attacks of predators. The predators are more easily pushed away by the group. Furthermore, as is the case of the large flocks of migrating birds, the large number of birds greatly reduces the chances for a single bird to be attacked.

One of the more familiar birds in Japan is the Japanese crane. This species is now threatened with extinction. It survives in small colonies in Siberia, China, and the eastern part of the island of Hokkaido. This last region is the marshy zone of Kucharo, near Kushiro. The Japanese crane is about 5 feet (1.5 m) tall. It is characterized by a contrasting black-and-white plumage, with a red crest on the head. It is a symbol of joy and happiness. According to a legend, it is destined to live for one thousand years. The Japanese crane is a figure that is frequently found in literature, art, and mythology.

The mating rituals of the Japanese cranes are impressive, occurring anytime between January and March. The male and the female bow while moving their wings and walking around each other with small steps. As the courtship proceeds, the excitement gradually builds. The partners begin to move faster, jumping and moving their wings rapidly. They even hover in the air at a height of from 6 to 10 feet (2 to 3 m). The pair often remains united for long periods of time.

After courtship, the mated pair returns to the same nesting site of the previous year. Here it builds a tall nest of grass and branches. Two eggs are usually laid, and the male and female take turns brooding them (keeping them warm). The chicks hatch at the end of April or at the beginning of May. At first they are very awkward. However, by the end of the summer they have nearly completed the growth of their white feathers. Several brown young feathers may remain on the head and the neck until the end of the first winter.

The Japanese crested ibis is another bird with a long neck and legs. One hundred years ago, it nested in vast areas of eastern Asia. However, it has now become extremely rare. Up until the early 1900s, this ibis was still common in Japan.

Today, only a few birds of this species remain, and they

The Japanese crane is a unique bird. It winters in the snowy northern parts of Japan and can withstand temperatures below 32°F (0°C). The Asian populations of this species nest in the Amur region of Mongolia and in Manchuria. Unlike their Japanese relatives, during the winter, they migrate to the nonsnowy regions of Korea and China.

are found mostly on the island of Sado. Fortunately, the Japanese crested ibis also inhabits some regions of China. This bird has a white-and-pink plumage and a black beak that curves downward. The face and the legs are red. The crested ibis is highly valued in Japan for its beautiful reddish pink feathers. The Japanese crested crane prefers to nest on very high trees. The great amount of tree cutting is one of the causes of its decline. Recently, a reserve was created to protect this ibis on more than 2,470 acres (1,000 hectares) of land on the island of Sado.

Numerous perching birds nest in Japan. The watered meadows surrounding Lake Tofutsu, on the island of Hokkaido, have a beautiful spring blooming season. These meadows are an important environment for the migratory birds. One of the most common migratory birds is the Siber-

ian thrush. The male of this species is characterized by a scarlet throat. Other summer migrators include several species of buntings, such as the collared bunting and the reed bunting. Various species of grasshopper warblers are common. Their high-pitched singing at dawn and dusk resembles the chirping of crickets.

On the island of Honshu, the rare Japanese marsh warbler nests in a similar marshy environment in the Aomori Province. The mountain forests of Hokkaido are inhabited by pine grosbeaks. The three-toed woodpecker and the green woodpecker are also found on this island. The grosbeaks have short cone-like beaks. They feed on seeds, berries, and shoots. The woodpeckers use their beaks to make holes in the tree bark. They capture insects in the wood by pulling them out with long, thin tongues.

Another rare bird with brilliant colors is the Pryer's woodpecker. It is found only in the subtropical forests of broadleaf trees on the peninsula of Okinawa. This species was first described in 1887. It is particularly interesting to biologists (those who study plants and animals) since it is the only species of its genus. It is impossible to mistake the Pryer's woodpecker for any other species of woodpecker. The Pryer's woodpecker has a brown body, a red back, a pink underside, and three white bands on the wings.

Mount Chokai, on the island of Honshu, is famous for the large variety of birds it hosts. Some of them are Eurasian species. Examples are the alpine accentor, the thick-billed nutcracker, the Japanese blue flycatcher (typical of eastern Asia), and the colorful Narcissus flycatcher. The flycatchers feed mainly on insects, especially flies, which they capture in flight. The black paradise flycatcher captures insects on the ground. It has extremely long tail feathers and a white underside. The rest of the plumage is black with dark red reflections.

The lesser cuckoo and the Himalayan cuckoo nest further south, on Mount Hiei. They are found with the Japanese green woodpecker and the varied tit. The varied tit is exclusive to Japan, and it is similar to the coal tit. However, it is distinguished by a white-and-black striped marking on the head, an orange breast, and black wings.

Mammals

Compared to the great number of bird species that live in Japan, the mammal species are relatively few, numbering ninety land-dwelling species. These include the mammal

Following pages: The Asiatic black bear is widely distributed in Asia. It inhabits regions ranging from the Himalayas and Mongolia to Burma and Indochina. The Japanese black bear is smaller than the brown bear, its continental relative. The characteristic white collar is not as evident on the Japanese variety. The Asiatic black bear has strong front legs and is a skillful tree climber. Its diet is varied, although it is mainly vegetarian.

species that were introduced and later naturalized. The Taiwan macaque and the nutria are examples of introduced species. The nutria, which is a large beaverlike rodent, originated in South America. It was imported into Japan to be raised on ranches for its fur. Several nutrias escaped into the wild from the ranches. They inhabited the rice paddies where they soon began to reproduce successfully. Today, the nutria is especially common in the Province of Okayama, in the southern part of the island of Honshu. Another introduced species is the masked palm civet. This mammal originated in the subtropical forests of southern Asia. Although it is rarely sighted, this civet had caused great damage to the orange orchards in the Province of Shizuoka.

Five large species of mammals live in Japan. Two of them are carnivores, or meat-eaters. They are the brown bear and the Asiatic black bear. The other three species are hoofed mammals—the sika deer, the Formosa serow, and the European wild boar. Besides the bears, other carnivores include the Iriomote cat and the raccoon dog.

The brown bears can reach a height of 10 feet (3 m). They inhabit the forests of Hokkaido up to 5,576 feet (1,700 m) of elevation. These bears either live alone or in family groups. The brown bears feed on berries, shoots, and roots. They also eat voles, pikas, freshwater crayfish, salmon, and trout. In the summer, the brown bears eat large amounts of food and build up large fat reserves. They hibernate in natural shelters between the rocks or in large dens.

The Asiatic black bear is slightly smaller than the brown bear. It is commonly called the "moon bear," as it has a white half-moon spot on its breast. This bear is relatively common in the northern part of Honshu. It usually wanders in search of food at night, spending the day asleep in a cave or in a large den.

The Iriomote cat got its name from the island it inhabits. It was described as a distinct species only thirty years ago. The Japanese government has taken steps to protect this animal, which is estimated to number from 120 to 130 individuals. The Iriomote cat is slightly larger than a domestic cat, with a brownish yellow coat spotted with black. It lives in evergreen forests, where it roams at night in search of prey such as birds, rodents, and insects.

The raccoon dog measures about 2 feet (60 cm) from head to tail. It has, especially in winter, a long, thick brownish yellow fur. Its name comes from the black pattern

The raccoon dog was originally found in Japan, eastern Siberia, northern China, and Manchuria. However, about sixty years ago it was introduced into the northern part of Russia. From there it spread west as far as Germany. The raccoon dog is a nocturnal forest animal that usually lives alone. The young are born in a den that is either dug by the mated male and female or has been abandoned by other animals. The litters contain from two to ten young, although litters of four to six are most common. The raccoon dog eats both plants and animals, including small vertebrates, insects, eggs, and berries.

around and below the eyes, which resembles the mask of a raccoon. Originally from eastern Asia, the raccoon dog lives in forests and prefers to stay close to bodies of water. At night it hunts rodents and fish. Its diet also includes fruits. It spends the day sheltered among rocks or in tree cavities. On Hokkaido island, the winters are very cold. Thus, like the brown bear, the raccoon dog hibernates until the following spring.

The sika deer originated in Japan and eastern Asia. Different-sized varieties are found on the various Japanese islands. The largest varieties, which also have the longest and most impressive horns, inhabit the northernmost islands. The sika is much less social than the common deer, to which it is closely related.

The Formosa serow is a goatlike antelope. It measures about 3 feet (1 m) in height. It is smaller than the Sumatran serow, which lives in China and Southeast Asia. The hair of the Formosa serow is longer and woolier than that of the Sumatran serow. Its coat varies in color from dark gray to reddish brown. The Formosa serow is an able climber. It inhabits grasslands and pine woods up to elevations of about 3,280 feet (1,000 m).

The sika deer lives in the forests of various Japanese islands at elevations higher than 8,200 feet (2,500 m). The antlers of this species are simpler than those of the European red deer. The sika deer is a wary animal. It becomes alarmed at the least hint of danger. When alarmed, this animal raises the hair of the hind parts.

The Formosa serow is one of the numerous Japanese native species. Other native mammals inhabit the southernmost islands of Japan. Among these are the Iriomote cat, the Ryukyu hare, and two species of fruit bats. Fruit bats are the largest species of bats. They are also called "flying foxes." This is not so much due to their size as it is to their reddish brown color and to the shape of their snouts, which resemble those of foxes. They have large eyes and small ears. The fruit bats lack a sonar (sounding) device. The insect-eating bats, however, all have a sonar or sound wave device they use to find prey. The fruit bats do not live in caves. They sleep during the day while hanging from tree branches like large black fruits. The clustered groups of sleeping fruit bats can number into the tens of thousands.

The Ryukyu hare lives exclusively on two islands of the Japanese archipelago. It has a thick fur that is dark brown on the back, reddish on the sides, and light on the underside. It is a primarily nocturnal animal. The Ryukyu hare spends the day inside a den. It comes out at night to feed on grasses and, above all, the tender shoots of ferns. Little is known of its reproductive biology. The female bears only one litter per year. Before becoming a protected species in 1921,

Japanese macaques are known for their great ability to transmit personal experiences and learned behaviors from one individual to the next. Zoologists have observed and studied this species, under natural conditions, for many years. Their conclusions show that the Japanese macaques have a highly developed level of communication between individuals. Furthermore, they have a complex social organization with a ranking system, and unusual sexual behavior and family relations.

this hare was widely hunted. Unfortunately, the cutting down of its forest environments and attacks by packs of wild dogs have further reduced its populations.

The Japanese dormouse and the Japanese macaque are two more native species. They are distributed over all the territory of Honshu, Shikoku, and Kyushu. The Japanese dormouse is a rodent that greatly resembles the common dormouse. It has a soft olive brown fur with a black stripe on the back. This animal inhabits forests up to an elevation of

Japanese dormouse

5,904 feet (1,800 m). The Japanese dormouse hides during the day in tree cavities. It comes out at night to search for seeds and fruits. During the summer, it builds a spherical nest among tree branches. Here it raises its litter, which is usually composed of three offspring. As winter draws near, the rodent looks for a den in a tree trunk or under the roof of a house. It hibernates here until spring.

The Japanese macaque is a rather large monkey with thick hair. It has a long, sad face that is pink in color. The Japanese macaque lives in social groups that often consist of more than one hundred individuals. The species mainly inhabits forests with mild climates. However, several populations are found in the subarctic forests north of Honshu, where snowfall is abundant. No other monkey populations in the world live this far north.

The Japanese macaques have a great learning capacity and are quick at picking up new ideas. Once a group of these macaques discovered some volcanic hot springs. Several of the animals became curious and found out that the hot water provided ideal conditions for hot baths during the winter. The habit of taking hot baths soon began to spread among the other monkeys. Now all the monkeys of the group take hot baths during the winter. Curiosity and the ability to adapt are typical behavioral traits of macaques. This enables these animals to easily adopt new activities as customary habits.

An episode that happened in another group of macaques on the island of Koshima shows this ability more clearly. The Koshima group had been studied by a group of researchers since 1952. To get closer to the monkeys, the researchers attracted them with sweet potatoes. Once a young female called "Imo" washed away the sand from her potato before eating it. This behavior quickly spread among the group. Today, the habit of washing the potatoes in the sea before eating them is more or less an accepted practice. The only macaques that have not learned are the older ones that are too rooted in their ways to make a change.

THE TIBETAN PLATEAU, THE STEPPES, THE DESERTS

Mongolia and northwestern China lie south of the Altai and Sayan mountains. These are vast regions of plains and plateaus, of desert and semidesert. There are large areas of land lying at elevations between 6,560 and 9,840 feet (2,000 and 3,000 m). One of the most arid zones is occupied by the Gobi Desert, one of the largest deserts in the world. Further south is the extensive Tibetan plateau. Its mountains reach an average elevation of 13,120 feet (4,000 m). Several peaks are from 19,680 to 22,960 feet (6,000 to 7,000 m) in elevation. This region includes the great plains of Chang Tang and the arid plateaus of central Tibet. The massive mountain chains of Kunlun are to the north and the Himalayas to the south.

Climate

In the alpine (mountainous) zone above the tree limit, and in the steppes and desert plains, the animals and plants must adapt to the great seasonal changes in temperature. In Mongolia, the average temperature in January is about -31°F (-35°C) in the north and 14°F (-10°C) in the south. The summer is short and relatively warm. The average temperatures range from 64° to 79°F (18° to 26°C). At Gartok, on the Tibetan plateau, the average temperature in January is 11°F (-12°C), while in July it is about 53°F (12°C).

Besides the alternation of relatively warm summers with very cold winters, this region is also characterized by great daily differences in temperature. The organisms that live here must adapt to night temperatures in the 32°F (0°C) range, even when the days are relatively warm.

At high elevations, the air is much less dense than at lower levels. Consequently, the sun heats the air less here than at lower elevations. The radiation at the soil level, however, is much more intense. Thus, the temperature of the soil is higher than the temperature of the surrounding air. This warmer climatic zone at the soil level allows animals and plants to survive the extreme alpine conditions.

The alpine zone and the desert zones are characterized by an extreme scarcity of water. Northern Mongolia receives only 7.5 to 11 inches (200 to 300 mm) of rain per year. The extreme southern part receives less than 3.75 inches per year (100 mm). In the eastern part of the Tibetan plateau, the annual rainfall varies from 9 to 28 inches (250 to 750 mm). The far western part is drier. Although in several mountain zones the precipitation is more abundant, the greater part of the water is locked in the forms of ice or snow. Conse-

Opposite page: To the south, the cold and inhospitable regions of central Asia are bordered by the impressive Himalaya mountain chain. Its peaks reach the highest elevations in the world. The landscape is characterized by deep V-shaped valleys. These narrow valleys were cut into the rocks by the meltwater of the vast glaciers found at higher elevations. The photograph was taken near Kuldi in Nepal. It shows a typical example of a narrow valley, with Mount Machapuchare in the background.

47

Even the most barren landscapes can be interesting for the attentive traveler. This photograph was taken in the region of Dong Sheng in Inner Mongolia. It shows a deeply eroded valley with interesting shapes of rock pinnacles (pointed formations). The scarcity of vegetation is due to the climate, the instability of the terrain, and the grazing of goats. Goats are the only domestic animals that can be raised in these poor lands.

quently, this water is unavailable for the majority of the year. All these factors result in a short growing season for the vegetation.

The animals of these regions must also protect themselves against violent winds. These winds raise up snow in the mountains and sand in the deserts. At the highest elevations, the air is so thin that it is difficult to breathe. Therefore, the animal species living there must be able to adapt to a lower amount of oxygen in the blood.

Hoofed Animals

Most of the large animals that live in the alpine zones of the Tibetan plateau and in the mountain chains are hoofed animals. Examples are the yak, the chiru, wild horses, sheep, and goats. These hoofed animals are all herbivores (plant-eaters). They have molar teeth that are used to chew plant food. Their keen vision and group habits help them avoid the attacks of predators.

A thick winter fur protects them against the sharp differences in temperature. The fur is replaced by a lighter coat in the summer. The summer and winter coats have different colors, each one blending with the colors of the environment. This makes the animals almost invisible to predators.

The barren Chang Tang is a series of plateaus in northern Tibet. This area is the last main refuge of the wild yak and the chiru, which is similar to an antelope. In the nineteenth century, numerous herds of wild yaks were found in an area ranging from western Turkestan to China. However, in recent years the yak population has sharply declined. The competition with herds of cattle and domestic yaks for alpine pastures has driven the wild yaks even higher into the mountains. They can live at an elevation of up to 20,000 feet (6,100 m). This altitude is the highest elevation reached by a mammal species. The wild yak can also reach a considerable size. Females weigh more than 660 pounds (300 kg). The huge males are at least 6.5 feet (2 m) at the shoulder and weigh between 1,100 and 1,980 pounds (500 and 900 kg). The yak has a long snout, powerful shoulders, and short, stout legs.

The very large lungs of yaks enable them to take in enough oxygen from the thin mountain air. In the winter, they are covered by a thick, soft, wooly fur. In the spring, large tufts of this fur are shed. The new coat is a rougher black hair. The hair on the lower parts of the yak hangs down to the ground. The strong hooves are well suited to the roughness of the terrain.

The tongue of the yak has small and hard nipplelike projections. These enable the animal to feed on short grasses, which can be tough and extremely hard to pull from the ground. For most of the year, the females and the young live in herds consisting of from twenty to two hundred individuals. The males usually live alone. In the spring, the new growth of grasses attracts large groups of yaks.

The delicate-looking chiru measures only about 3 feet

(1 m) at the shoulder. It is characterized by a pale brown coat. The males have long and slender dark horns that are used when charging a rival male during fights. These fights are often bloody and sometimes result in the deaths of both males from the goring of their horns. As a protection against the severe environment and ceaseless winds, the chirus take shelter in holes in the ground. The young are born in May.

The chirus have a small, pointed snout similar to that of the saiga of the Russian steppes and the Gobi Desert. Both the chiru and the saiga have cavities inside the nostrils that enable them to heat and humidify the dry, cold air as soon as it is inhaled.

The bharal sheep is another hoofed mammal species that lives in the alpine pastures above the tree limit. The wool on its head and back is of a brownish gray color with silver blue shades. This coloring makes the animal clearly visible against the background of rocks. During the summer, the bharal sheep loses large tufts of its winter coat.

The bharal sheep are as agile as goats. They are able to climb rougher and steeper slopes than any other sheep.

The wild yak is the largest animal of the cold Tibetan plateau. It was described for the first time only a century ago by the famous Russian explorer Nikolai Przewalski. At that time, the herds of wild yaks were numerous. Since then, however, their numbers have been greatly reduced. One of the reasons for this decline is the greater number of domestic yak (in the photograph) that compete for grazing land. The domestic yak is smaller than the wild yak.

50

The interesting and unique *Saussurea leucocoma (top)* is one of the plants that has adapted to the high elevations and harsh conditions of the Tibetan plateau. It is scattered here and there among the wind-blown soil. The cottony covering that wraps the plant protects it from losing too much heat and moisture. A small opening here at the top of this covering enables bees to enter and pollinate the flowers. The Himalayan star, *Leontopodium stracheyi (bottom),* has woolly leaves that protect the small flower heads. These protective leaves resemble flower petals.

Thus, they graze on the edges of steep cliffs and slopes. During the summer, they live in herds of from thirty to one hundred individuals. One of them often serves as a sentry or guard. Wolves or snow leopards are the main predators of the bharal sheep. The adult males often remain alone at higher elevations. Mating occurs in November or December. Usually one male dominates a small group of females.

The argali is the largest wild sheep. At least fifteen varieties of this species are known. They all inhabit the highest mountains of central Asia. The most notable of these is the Marco Polo's sheep, which lives in the Pamir Mountains of south central Asia and in the western Himalayas. It has a gray coat that is protected in winter by a long white fur that covers its neck, shoulders, and breast. The Marco Polo's sheep is about 4 feet (1.3 m) at the shoulder and weighs more than 350 pounds (160 kg). The males have large, ribbed horns of an iron gray color. The horns curve backward and form a complete circle before pointing outward. The longest horns of this species have been recorded at 4 feet (120 cm). The mating season lasts from December to the beginning of January.

In the spring, the winter herds of argalis break up and the older females guide small groups of a dozen young to the summer pastures. In these barren lands, the argalis can more easily flee from the wolf, their main enemy.

The largest variety of argali sheep is the Tibetan sheep, which is characterized by a brown coat. The Tibetan sheep is found further west, across the Tibetan plateau toward Mongolia. The males have a white collar and horns that spiral outward. Although the horns are shorter than those of the Marco Polo's sheep, their spread is greater than a person's arms. Little is known of these animals. According to the Mongolian nomads of the Altai Mountains, the majority of the herds move to the bottom of the valley during winter. In the spring, they are said to graze on the steep banks of mountain streams. They gradually move higher into the mountains as the snow melts. The birth of the lambs occurs between May and June. After the birth of the young, the males climb to an elevation of 19,352 feet (5,900 m), to the limit of the vegetation. Here they gather in herds of sixty or more. They prefer to graze in the early morning and at dusk.

The plateau of central Tibet extends south of Chang Tang. This area is inhabited by a wild ass called the "kiang," of which five Asian varieties still exist. The wild asses are stocky animals, with large lungs and strong hind legs. The

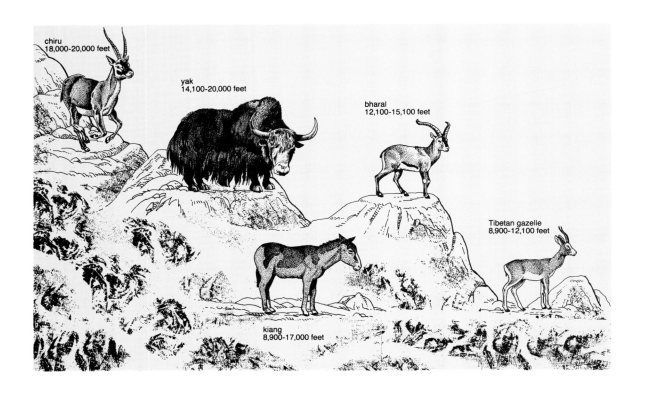

chiru
18,000-20,000 feet

yak
14,100-20,000 feet

bharal
12,100-15,100 feet

Tibetan gazelle
8,900-12,100 feet

kiang
8,900-17,000 feet

The illustration shows several of the hoofed animals and the elevations at which they are found in the steppes, highlands, and plateaus of Tibet. The chiru is still numerous, forming large herds. The yak, on the other hand, has a low population of isolated individuals.

legs are adapted for running. The animals have long ears and small, extremely hard hooves. The varieties of wild asses differ slightly in color and size. The coat is usually of a uniform reddish brown or sandy color, with a whitish underside. A black stripe runs along the back, from the mane to the tail. Like zebras, wild asses survive on sparse pastureland. They also eat scattered shrubs. Their distribution seems to be limited by the availability of water. In the winter, when snow and water puddles are abundant, the asses spread out over a vast territory. They are also spread out over large areas in the spring, when new grass grows everywhere. During the dry summer season, when the drinking locations are more scarce, the herds rarely move more than a couple miles away from water. An animal cannot survive for more than two or three days without water.

At one time, the chigetai lived in part of Mongolia, Manchuria, and Chinese Turkestan. The distribution area of this species gradually became smaller over the last 2,000 years. The chigetai presently lives only in the southern and southwestern regions of Mongolia. This animal is as fast as a racehorse and has an amazing endurance. It is able to maintain a speed of 25 to 30 miles (40 to 48 km) per hour for

The Mongolian wild horse is the last surviving species of wild horses. European wild horses became extinct in the last century. The future of the Mongolian wild horse seems uncertain. Information on its survival in the wild is lacking. Perhaps the survival of the species will be tied to the breeding of specimens living in zoos.

several hours. The colts are able to stand on their legs on the same day they are born. This ability allows them to flee the attacks of the wolf, their main predator.

Since herds of chigetais are very wary, it is extremely difficult to approach them in the open. Before firearms were introduced into the area, the only possible way to bring down these animals was by careful ambushes. After the introduction of firearms, the populations of chigetais were greatly reduced. Their hides and meat brought a good price on the market. Today, the chigetai is protected both in Tibet and Mongolia. Its survival seems to be assured by the environments it inhabits, which are extremely difficult to approach.

The Mongolian wild horse was discoverd in 1870 by the Russian naturalist Nikolai Przewalski. It is the only surviving variety of wild horses.

The Mongolian wild horse is slightly smaller than the domestic horse. It has a short, erect mane and lacks the typical tuft of hair on the forehead. At one time, its distribution area probably extended from the Altai Mountains to western Mongolia and to the edges of the border with China.

Today the Mongolian wild horse is strictly protected. It survives only in the mountainous and semidesert region of the Taklin Shar-nuru Mountains in southwestern Mongolia. It moves each season in search of pastures in the Gobi Desert or toward China. It is difficult to observe this animal in the wild because of the difficulty of reaching locations in which it lives, its constant wariness, and its ability to flee in an instant. Six of these wild horses were seen in 1966 in Mongolia, and more were later seen. About two hundred fifty of these animals presently live in zoos. The zoo of Prague, Czechoslovakia keeps a world register of the pedigrees of the species in the hope of saving it from extinction.

The camel has been used for centuries by humans in central Asia as a beast of burden. Its meat and skin are also valued. For many years, it was thought that all camels existing in the wild had become exctinct. Wild camels had

The Gobi Desert is a vast expanse covering a large part of Outer Mongolia and the neighboring parts of Inner Mongolia, in Chinese territory. Most of the desert's scarce streams do not flow toward the sea. In fact, there is a sort of basin at an average elevation of 2,950 feet (900 m), surrounded by mountains that largely reach elevations of 6,560 feet (2,000 m) and beyond. The average annual rainfall in the Gobi Desert is less than 7.5 inches (190 mm). In the interior parts, this average is less than 1.8 inches (46 mm). There is a great difference in temperatures between winter and summer. The winter low can reach -40°F (-40°C) and the summer high can reach 100°F (38°C). The animal and plant life is very limited in this region. Naturally, the highest concentrations of plants and animals are found in the wetland areas.

been mentioned in the ancient Chinese literature until the fifth century, althouth mention of these animals was also made in the writings of Marco Polo in the thirteenth century. In 1879, Przewalski spotted several wild camels around Lake Lob, southeast of the Gobi Desert. The local people told Przewalski that wild camels were numerous at one time. They had been hunted for their meat and skins up until several decades before his visit. Today only one population of wild camels survives, made up of from 400 to 500 animals, living in the southwestern part of Mongolia.

Pikas and Woodchucks

In the mountains, above the tree limit, the mammals are represented mostly by rodents, hares, rabbits, and pikas. Some of the rodents are woodchucks, jerboas, gerbils, and voles. All these animals have soft, thick fur, which protects

long-eared jerboa

brush-toed jerboa

fat-tailed jerboa

great jerboa

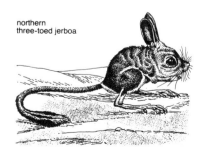

northern three-toed jerboa

them from the cold. Most of these animals live in dens, where some species hibernate through the winter.

The pikas are also known as "whistling hares." Their nickname comes from the type of calls they make to communicate with other pikas or to warn of possible danger. The pikas resemble rabbits. However, their ears are shorter, and they are no larger than a guinea pig. Pikas have rounded snouts with whiskers. The ears are completely protected by a thick brownish gray fur. In Asia there are twelve species of pikas. In the Himalayas, pikas have been found on the slopes of Mount Everest at elevations higher than 17,384 feet (5,300 m).

Pikas do not hibernate through the winter. To prepare for the long cold spell, they stockpile straw at the end of the summer. They are able to cover distances of many hundreds of yards from their dens to gather grasses. They transport the bundles of grass with the mouth to suitable locations for drying. Layers of fresh grass accumulate with repeated trips, with the pile sometimes reaching a height of 22 inches (60 cm). The straw is then stored.

Like the hares and rabbits, the pikas "redigest" their food, chewing and swallowing then throwing up. The small balls of food thrown up during the day are green and dry. Those thrown up at night are kept moist by a covering of mucous. These balls of food ferment as they are exposed to the air, becoming enriched in essential vitamins. When the food balls are eaten again, they have a higher nutrient level. This habit enables the pikas to make the maximum use of their food. Without this habit, the pikas would die of starvation in the winter after a period of three weeks.

In the high-elevation grasslands of Tibet, several birds live in friendly relationships with the pikas. Some examples are crows, alpine accentors, and snow finches. In fact, these birds nest in the dens of the pikas and feed on the grass seeds that are strewn about the entrances.

Marmots (woodchucks) are heavy animals with short legs. They are able to run, jump, and climb among the rocks with a surprising agility and speed. Their rough, thick fur is dull in color. It varies from brownish red on the back to light gray or rust-colored on the underside.

The Altai marmot and the steppe marmot are the two most common species. Their habits are similar. The Altai marmot reaches a length of 22 inches (60 cm) and has a furry tail, about 5.5 inches (15 cm) long. During the summer, Altai marmots live on the spurs of the Himalayas and other

Malayan sun bear

Pallas' cat

snow leopard

Eurasian mountains. In this season they are found at elevations between 5,904 feet (1,800 m) and the limit of the perennial (year-round) snow.

Marmots live in small colonies, formed by an old male, eight females, and two young males, occupying separate dens. In the morning, it is easy to observe them basking in the sun while a sentry watches out for possible danger. At the least sign of danger, the sentry regularly repeats a long, shrill whistle to alert all the members of the colony. When they hear this whistle, they immediately rush into the den.

Marmots are herbivores. They feed on grasses and roots that they gnaw with their strong incisor (front, biting) teeth. They often spend time cleaning themselves and playing. In Mongolia, they have been observed scratching each other with the front paws and making dancing movements. As the summer wears on, the marmots become fatter, and when the bad weather arrives they start digging their winter dens.

The Snow Leopard

The predators of the alpine zone include sand-colored foxes with bushy tails and large ears. They also include wolves, which prey mostly on antelope and gazelles. The Malayan sun bear also inhabits this zone. This animal has brownish black fur, grizzled with gray or silver tones. One of the smallest predators of this zone is the Pallas' cat, which has a light gray coat. The most beautiful predator of this zone is the snow leopard, which is also the most difficult to observe. The snow leopard has become rare in its area of distribution, which ranges from the Pamir region to the Tibetan plateau, Tien Shan, the Altai Mountains, and the Sayan Mountains.

The snow leopard is smaller than the common leopard. It measures slightly over 4 feet (1.3 m) in height at the shoulder. It is easily identified by the enormous paws, the thick 3-foot (1-m) long tail, and the thick, velvety fur. Its coat is of a dull silver gray color. Blackish spots and rosettes (formation resembling a rose) form a pattern that allows this animal to easily camouflage itself. Most of the surviving snow leopards live on the wild slopes of the Himalayas. They also inhabit barren snowy lands and alpine grasslands at high elevations. In these areas, the snow leopard preys on a wide variety of mammals, including bharal sheep, young yaks, marmots, and pikas.

The European redstart is related to the nightingale and the robin, and is widespread in Eurasia. The male and female of this species have remarkable differences. The male has brighter colors, with a black throat and brick red breast. The plumage of the female is characterized primarily by brown tones. Both male and female have a red tail. The redstart usually nests in tree cavities. It hunts insects in a manner similar to that of the flycatcher.

ibis-beak

white-crowned forktail

Himalayan snow grouse

red-billed chough

Birds of the High Himalayas

The Asiatic dipper bird inhabits the areas near the mountain streams of the Himalayas. It is often seen jumping and diving into the clear water to capture water beetles and snails. One of the adaptations associated with its peculiar habits is its soft, shiny plumage. The plumage covers a thick layer of skin glands that produce fatty substances necessary to waterproof the feathers.

The ibis-bill is another aquatic bird that feeds in the calm pools of fast-flowing mountain streams. It has long legs and a grayish plumage and resembles the European avocet. This bird searches for prey among the rocks. Its red beak is long and slender and curves downward. The ibis-bill is found in mountain streams up to an elevation of 14,500 feet (4,400 m). It nests in ancient glacial valleys above 9,800 feet (3,000 m) of elevation.

The white-crowned forktail can also be seen jumping and zig-zagging among the rock masses in the middle of the water current. This bird searches for aquatic larvae and insects in the water. It resembles a black wagtail, not only for its black-and-white coloring, but also for the continuous up and down movement of the deeply forked tail.

The snow pigeon rarely descends below an elevation of 4,920 feet (1,500 m). Flocks of these birds come down from the mountains every morning to feed in the potato fields between the houses of the Sherpas (local people of the Himalayas). Often they are also seen in the higher cultivated valleys. At night, the snow pigeons return to their refuges. These are located on the high rock walls beyond the limit of the perennial snow. The golden eagle, their main predator, cannot follow them to this elevation.

The white-and-gray snow grouses resemble large partridges. These large birds weigh at least 5.5 pounds (2.5 kg). In the morning, they glide down into the valleys. After having drunk water in a lake, they return to the steep slopes above an elevation of 20,000 feet (6,100 m). Here the snow grouses spend the day digging for roots. Snow grouses are common in a large part of the central Asian mountains, above 8,856 feet (2,700 m) of elevation. Their long, echoing calls are well known.

The shiny black choughs belong to the crow family. Both the red-billed chough and the alpine chough inhabit the cliffs and villages of the Himalayas. They are also found in the other rocky mountains of Eurasia. They can be seen flying alone or in flocks. Both species are known for their

Pictured are gulls on the island of Niao Dao in Lake Qinghai, northeast of the Qinghai Province in central-western China. This enormous lake covers 2,309 sq. miles (5,980 sq. km) and is found at an elevation of about 10,500 feet (3,200 m). The lake is 328 feet (100 m) deep, has no rivers flowing out of it, and is iced over from November to March. Due to the summer rains, an abundant food supply for animals is produced along the low and marshy shores. The gulls are attracted by the abundance of food in the marshes and in the lake. They establish numerous colonies along the shores. The diet of the gulls is varied. Besides fish, they also readily eat small mammals, bird eggs, and refuse.

The bearded vulture feeds on carcasses of domestic and wild animals. Flying high above, it scouts vast areas of territory in search of carcasses that have already been stripped by the griffon vulture. The bearded vulture grabs a large bone and flies high to drop it on rocks. Thus the bone is broken open, and the vulture can feed on the precious marrow.

acrobatic flight. They make all sorts of flying maneuvers around the peaks on which they live. They spiral upward and then dive straight downward. Then they regain altitude once more and fan out from the flock formation with the wings closed or open.

The habitat of the red-billed chough ranges from an elevation of 4,920 feet (1,500 m) during the winter, to 7,872 to 16,072 feet (2,400 to 4,900 m) during the spring and summer. In the summer, it nests on roofs and in the walls of houses in high mountain villages. Red-billed choughs also live in holes or in the cracks of inaccessible rocks.

The magnificent bearded vultures often fly very high in search of sheep and yak carcasses. With a wingspan of 8.5 feet (2.6 m), they are able to go beyond mountain passes or fly low to the ground while rarely beating their wings. Like all vultures, they feed on animal carcasses.

A pair of bearded vultures usually occupies a large territory, seldom leaving it. They build a nest of branches, bones, and animal hair on an inaccessible rock ledge or in a cavity.

The Himalayan griffon vulture is common almost everywhere in the Himalayas. It lives at higher elevations than the bearded vulture, often reaching 20,000 feet (6,100

m). Unlike the bearded vulture, the Himalayan griffon vulture nests in communities with other nesting pairs. It is not unusual for fifty pairs to be nesting in the same cavern or on the same rock ledge. They also eat in groups on the same carcasses.

The birds of prey are not the only birds that can be seen among the highest peaks of the world. The bar-headed geese have been observed flying above 25,919 feet (7,900 m) of elevation. These flights occur when the geese migrate from the lake region of the Indian plains, where they winter, to the Tibetan plateau.

The ruddy sheldrake ducks are other migratory birds that nest near the lakes. They inhabit areas up to an elevation of 16,076 feet (4,900 m). Their calls are loud and melodious. In these environments, one can also hear the sad call of the wood snipe. In July and August, common gulls can occasionally be seen fishing in the lakes. Where the rivers flow into the larger lakes, one can also find the Pallas' fishing eagle. This eagle surveys the surface of the water, searching for prey from high above.

The bar-headed goose is widespread in central Asia, from the Pamir mountain region to Mongolia. During the course of its migrations, it crosses the Himalaya mountain chain, flying at altitudes of over 26,240 feet (8,000 m).

butterfly of the *Parnassius* genus

butterfly of the *Baltia* genus

jumping spider

midge

springtail

scale insects of the *Adonia* genus

rove beetle

mayfly

stonefly

midge

jumping spider

earwig

centipede

ground beetles

pseudoscorpion

millipede

Invertebrate Animals of the High Mountains

Ants, bees, beetles, crickets, and other insects are among the most common invertebrates (animals without backbones) of the mountains. They inhabit areas up to an elevation of 16,400 feet (5,000 m). Many of them live under snow, rocks, and clumps of vegetation. Some are also found in the thin layer of soil. Within these tiny environments, they are subject to much less extreme temperatures than if they lived in the open. Furthermore, a larger amount of water is available in these environments.

In the majority of cases, the invertebrates feed in the early morning, before the soil becomes too dry. They are often dark colored. This enables them to better absorb the heat of the sun in a short period of time. Because of the extreme environmental conditions of the areas they inhabit, the invertebrates have evolved special adaptations. These include the highly reflective surfaces of the backs of pill bugs and the special wing cases of beetles. These surfaces protect them from the intense solar radiation. Another adaptation is the unusual hairiness of many flies, which limits their heat loss.

The Tibetan beetles of the *Pseudabris* genus feed on such legumes as peas, beans, and clovers. They are characterized by brilliant red and black stripes. As soon as a strong wind begins to blow, they immediatley drop to the ground as if they were dead. Only springtails, bristletails, tiny midgets, and jumping spiders are able to survive above an elevation of 16,076 feet (4,900 m). Bristletails are primitive insects often found in homes. Springtails are small insects of 0.197 inch (5 mm). They are wingless and have very primitive features. Springtails have forked tails, folded like a spring at the rear end of the body. When it is released, the tail hits the ground and vaults the insect into the air an inch or two (a few centimeters).

Bees and butterflies move up and down the mountains in search of flowers. The butterflies include various species of swallowtails and thistle butterflies. Butterflies of the genera *Baltia* and *Esperia* also are found in these mountains. The delicate-winged *Parnassius* acco lays its eggs at higher elevations than any other butterfly species.

The unusual scale insects of the *Adonis* genus move about in thick swarms on several peaks of the Himalayas. They spend the winter under the snow. These scale insects can reach population densities of twenty thoudand insects per square yard (16,700 per sq. m).

Opposite page: Only a few invertebrate species have adapted to the harsh environment of the highest peaks of the Himalayas. Their survival is based on resources that are invisible to the naked eye. These invertebrates sometimes multiply into numerous colonies. This is the case of the insects and spiders that live under rocks, such as jumping spiders, springtails, and midges. In these tiny environments, small fragments of food are transported and deposited by the wind. The invertebrates search for food (often composed of mosses and lichens) in the cracks of rocks and between stones. Some of the invertebrates are predators, such as the ground beetles.

THE SIBERIAN TAIGA AND LAKE BAIKAL

The name "taiga" is used to refer to the wide belt of largely conifer forests typical of the far northern latitudes. This forest belt crosses the whole Eurasian continent. It ranges from Scandinavia to the Sea of Okhost, the northwest arm of the Pacific Ocean. The Siberian taiga covers an area that is about one-third the size of the United States. At the southern edge of this forest lies Lake Baikal, the oldest lake in the world. It covers an area of over 11,966 sq. miles (31,000 sq. km).

Trees

The conifer trees are resistant and well adapted to a wide variety of environmental conditions. They are abundant in every region of the earth. However, in the taiga they reign supreme. The conifers reach the northern limit of their distribution in Siberia. Here the average temperatures in the summer months range from 55° to 66°F (13° to 19°C). In the winter, they easily drop below -40°F (-40°C).

Trees that grow in this environment must be able to withstand long periods of cold and dryness. The extremely low temperatures can cause the water to freeze inside plant tissues. At such cold temperatures, the water in the soil and above the soil is in the form of ice.

Wind and the snow can also be harmful to trees. Limbs can easily be broken off by their force. The trees must make all of their annual growth within a growing season that lasts for only three or four months. Furthermore, they must obtain their nutrients from extremely poor soils.

In the taiga, the abundant precipitation and the short growing season create a situation of unusually low water evaporation from the soil. The amount of water that returns to the atmosphere by evaporation is less than the amount of precipitation that reaches the soil in the form of rain and snow. As a result, the water in the soil moves mainly downward. This process is evident in the soils of the taiga. A thick layer of needles from the conifer trees accumulates on the top of the forest soil. The needles decompose slowly, forming a layer of acidic, broken-down plant matter (humus) just under the leaf litter. The acids in this layer are carried downward into the lower layers of the soil by the water received in the form of rain or snow. Through this process many important nutrients are carried downward, away from the reach of the tree roots. The nutrients are said to have been "leached" away by the water. The accumulation of mineral substances rich with iron forms a brownish red

Opposite page: The moose, which is the largest member of the deer family, is widely distributed in the taiga. Its main predators are bears and wolves. Wolverines also prey on young moose. It is not easy for these carnivores to bring down an adult moose, since this giant knowns how to defend itself. Besides the powerful antlers of the males, moose effectively use their front hooves as weapons. Wolves usually hunt moose in packs. Only a small percentage of their attacks meet with success.

An autumn landscape is seen along the Angara River in Siberia, not far from Lake Baikal.

layer in the soil. This layer slows the water drainage and obstructs the downward movement of tree roots.

Consequently, the root system of the conifers is shallow. The roots spread in a dense network near the soil surface, where nutrients are scarce. The low fertility of the soil is made up for by the presence of fungi. The fungi wrap the conifer roots with a tangle of thin vegetative threads. They take mineral salts from decomposing plants and animals and transfer these nutrients to the tree roots. In return, the fungi absorb carbohydrates (sugars and starches) from the tree roots. The fungi cannot produce these substances on their own. This mutual relationship, which is helpful to both the trees and the fungi is called "symbiosis."

Above ground, the conifers show further adaptations to the difficult environmental conditions. They are shaped like pyramids, with the branches leaning downward with respect to the trunk. This allows snow to easily slide off the branches. Since less snow accumulates on the branches, there is less chance that the branches will break from the snow's heavy weight. The needlelike leaves have a smaller surface, which is covered by a waxy layer. The reduced surface holds down water loss during the dry winter period. Almost all the conifer tree species are evergreen.

The larches lose their leaves every year, before winter sets in. The advantages of this are a lower water loss during the dry winter season and reduced damage due to wind and the piling up of snow. As a result of this adaptation, the larches are among the few tree species that manage to grow at as high an elevation as the tree line.

Conifer trees produce flowers and fruits on cones. Most of the conifer species produce male and female flowers on the same tree. The female flowers generally consist of small red spherical tufts. The tufts grow at the end of the shoots. The male flowers develop separately and produce immense clouds of yellow pollen. The pollen granules are transported by the wind across the forest, and they fertilize the female flowers.

The taiga can be divided into a light conifer forest and a dark conifer forest, according to the major vegetation. The dark conifer forest is characterized by spruces, firs, and pines. This forest grows in a taiga soil that is covered by a layer of mosses and lichens and by a thick layer of decomposing (rotting) needles. The trees that live in this type of

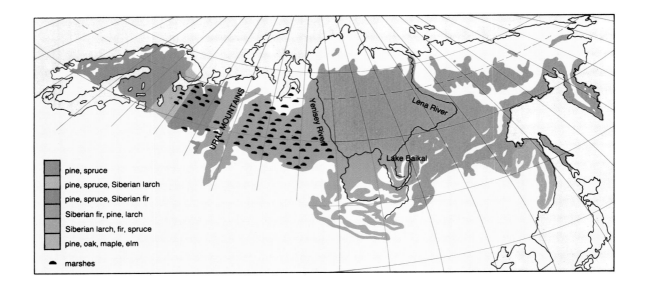

pine, spruce
pine, spruce, Siberian larch
pine, spruce, Siberian fir
Siberian fir, pine, larch
Siberian larch, fir, spruce
pine, oak, maple, elm
marshes

forest are able to grow close to each other. They manage to survive even in shady conditions. Their leaves can undergo the photosynthesis process even when little light is available. The small amount of light that reaches the soil of the forest hinders the growth of a normal underbrush. The underbrush is thus limited to several types of bushy plants. These include junipers, honeysuckles, viburnums, dwarf willows, blueberries, and cranberries.

The light conifer forest is dominated by larches and pines. This type of forest tends to be more open, the wider spaces between the trees allowing more light to reach the soil. Therefore, the underbrush of this forest is rather thick.

The conifer forests are rare in western Siberia. This region is rich with peat bogs and marshlands. One example is the vast Vasyugan marsh. These wet environments are formed as a result of poor drainage. Poor drainage is typical of the lowland zones, or floodplains, near streams and rivers. The excess water prevents the growth of trees. It does, however, result in the formation of a thick acidic layer of peat moss.

Birds

The most abundant and flavorful food produced by the taiga is the conifer seed. The majority of the animals do not feed on the waxy and resiny leaves of the conifer trees, although a few species of insects and birds are exceptions to this rule. Some of the year-round birds that feed on conifer

The Siberian taiga is the largest existing forest in the world. It is the realm of the conifer trees and is dotted with lakes, marshes, and ponds. Aspens, birches, and alders that are hardy enough to withstand the severe winter conditions grow here. The Yenisey River is the natural border dividing the two different regions of the taiga.

The bird's beak is a versatile instrument that can be adapted for various uses. Different types of beaks have been evolved for special purposes. The beak of the crossbills, for example, is crossed near the ends. This enables the crossbills to raise the scales of conifer cones and eat the seeds. This type of work sometimes requires acrobatic poses. Crossbills are often seen clinging to twigs and branches of the conifer trees, as in the photograph.

seeds are the brightly colored crossbills. The ends of these birds' beaks cross instead of uniting. The crossbills obtain seeds directly from the cone. They often use their strange-looking beak to cling to branches or to grasp objects.

The crossed beak is also used to open the scales of conifer cones vertically while the seed is quickly extracted with the tongue. In one day, a crossbill can collect and eat about one thousand of these high-protein seeds. The seeds of the cones that have fallen to the ground are also eaten. However, this is usually the case at the end of the winter or in spring, when food is not as plentiful.

Several species of crossbills inhabit the taiga. Each species has a slightly different beak, which is adapted for a particular type of pine cone. The red crossbill, for example, is specialized in opening the cones of the spruce and the larch. The pine crossbill, which has a heavier beak, eats

The thick-billed nutcracker belongs to a bird family that includes crows and magpies. It prefers conifer forests in mountainous regions. The nutcracker builds its nest in trees and lays two to five eggs, although three to four eggs are more commonly laid. Its diet consists of nuts, pine nuts, and other seeds and fruit. It often stores large amounts of food under the ground, which it is able to do even when the ground is covered by snow.

mainly the seeds of the harder pine cones.

One of the largest birds in this environment is the thick-billed nutcracker. This bird measures about 12 inches (30 cm) and has a dark brown plumage with scattered patches of white. The beak of this nutcracker is large and pointed. It is strong enough to break open the cones to remove the seeds.

The supply of seeds that the nutcrackers manage to stockpile in the fall is very important for this species. It is

important for their winter diet, and it also assures enough food for the young that are hatched during the following spring. In each nest, the number of young that reach maturity is directly related to the quality of conifer seeds produced in the previous growing season. The nutcrackers remember well the location of their food deposits. They are able to locate them even under a thick layer of snow.

The pine grosbeak resembles a large crossbill. However, its beak is straight, conical, and stout. This bird feeds on a wide variety of seeds and berries. It also eats conifer leaves, especially the young, tender shoots. In the spring, the female builds a nest of interlaced twigs. The nest is stuffed with soft roots, grass, and moss. The female lays four or five bluish green eggs, which she broods alone. However, the chicks are fed by both parents.

Another bird found year-round in the taiga is the capercaillie. This is the largest member of the grouse family. Although this species is not characterized by brilliant colors, the male is nevertheless an impressive bird. It is about 3 feet (1 m) long, with a bluish black back and gray stripes. It has a shiny greenish blue breast, red eyebrows, and a black "beard." The female is smaller and has pale colors. It is usually reddish with brown striping.

The capercaillie is a shy bird that often lives alone. This is especially true for the male. Like other grouse species, in the spring the male displays itself every morning for many weeks. This is done in an elaborate courtship ceremony. During this period, the male defends its small territory from intruders. The neck is held straight with the beak pointed upward, displaying the beard. The tail fans out as the male struts with small steps, making strange sounds and raising itself into flight now and then. This ceremony is performed to attract females. The females mate with the dominant males and then go off to build the nests.

At first, the young feed on small insects, soft berries, and young, tender shoots. But gradually, as they grow, they are able to digest needles and shoots of conifer trees. These make up the basic winter diet of this species.

The mountain francolin is a smaller bird belonging to the same family as the capercaillie. The male and female of this species are similar. They are brownish red in color with gray and white streaks. In the summer months, the mountain francolin feeds primarily on the ground. In winter, when the ground is covered with snow, it feeds almost exclusively in the conifer trees. Unlike the capercaillie, the

The black woodpecker is one of the stockiest species of its family. It can reach the size of a crow. Its diet consists mainly of wood-boring insects and ants. This bird takes wood-boring insects from the wood of old trees with the help of its long beak and very long tongue. The black woodpecker captures ants in the trees as well as on the ground.

The great gray owl prefers to inhabit the conifer forests of the northern regions of Asia and Europe. It is a large owl, comparable in size to the eagle owl. The great gray owl nests in the abandoned nests of other large birds. During the coldest winters, it flies south, beyond the normal area of its distribution.

mountain francolin lives in small groups. The groups break up only in the mating season, when mated pairs build their own nests and raise their chicks.

The woodpeckers are well represented in the conifer forests. The three-toed woodpecker and the black wood-pecker are especially common. They climb up tree trunks in search of insects. The insects are captured from cracks in the bark, or they are taken from the wood under the bark. The particular structure of their feet enables the wood-peckers to climb easily. The first and the fourth toes extend backward, while the second and third toes point forward. Of course, one of these toes is lacking in the three-toed wood-pecker. Furthermore, woodpeckers have sharp claws and rigid tail feathers, which serve to support the bird on tree trunks.

Some of the characteristic sounds of the forest are the drumming and tapping noises made by the beaks of these birds as they strike the tree trunks. The black woodpecker makes a truly loud noise, while the three-toed woodpecker pecks with a slower rhythm. The pecking of woodpeckers is done not only to search for food. It is also used as a mating call or to declare a territory.

The relative abundance of birds and rodents assures a good food supply for a wide variety of nonmigrating birds of prey. Among the most interesting owls are the great gray owl, the large-headed owl, the hawk owl, and the pygmy owl. The soft feathers of the owls enable them to fly quietly. Other characteristics are large heads and large eyes. The eyes are located forward on the head, much like the eyes of a person. As far as anyone knows, the owls are the only birds that have true three-dimensional vision. This is an important feature for a predator. It enables the owl to easily distinguish objects from the background. In addition, the owls have a great ability to locate the source of sounds. Thus, they can pounce on prey with great precision, even in complete darkness.

Each of the owl's eyes is encircled by a disk of fine feathers. These facial disks serve to channel the sounds toward the ears. These disks are particularly developed in the owls that hunt exclusively at night, such as the great gray owl. The ears of owls are not located in the same exact position on each side of the head. This difference in where the ears are placed results in a slightly different perception of sounds in the two ears. This slight difference enables the owls to locate the exact position of the prey.

hawk owl

thrush
(Turdus iliacus)

fieldfare

four-eyed duck
(Bucephala clangula) ♂

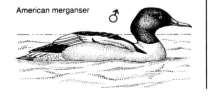

American merganser ♂

The great gray owl is one of the largest owls of the dense northern forests. It reaches a length of about 3 feet (1 m), and has a streaked dark gray plumage. The great gray owl nests in the abandoned nests of other larger birds of prey. Its diet consists mainly of voles. When the vole populations are low, the great gray owl lays only one or two eggs. However, when the voles increase in number, the broods also become more numerous. In certain years, up to seven eggs might be laid in one nest. The number of voles is related to the amount of food available. Their diet consists of conifer seeds, which are produced in varying amounts each year. Consequently, the vole population can decline suddenly, and when this occurs the great gray owls must migrate south in search of food.

The hawk owl is about half the size of the great gray owl. It is distinguished from other owls by the long tail and short, pointed wings. In flight, the peculiar wings give it the appearance of a hawk. This bold predator hunts mostly during the day. The bird attentively watches its hunting territory from a treetop.

One of the smallest owls is the pygmy owl. This species measures about 8 inches (20 cm) in length. It is partially active during the day, hunting small insects in flight. The pygmy owl occasionally nests in the holes of woodpeckers.

The cold conditions and the isolation of the taiga make it one of the least disturbed environments of the world. The summer is brief, but the days are longer during this period. A tremendous number of migratory birds fly here for the summer, attracted by the abundant insect food that is available to feed their young. The eggs and larvae of insects winter between the cracks of tree bark or in the leaf litter, under the thick blanket of snow. Eggs hatch and adults emerge from cocoons at the beginning of the summer. Numerous caterpillars crowd the new shoots of the conifers. The butterflies and flies enrich the forest with colors and sounds. Mosquitoes and midges raise up in thick swarms from the wetlands. Ants build mounds of dead needles on the forest floor. These mounds become homes for their queen and the numerous offspring of the colony. Flocks of thrushes and fieldfares arrive to feed on the caterpillars, while willow warblers and tits feed on adult insects. The migratory birds of prey also fly northward for the summer to prey on lemmings, voles, and small birds.

The goshawk arrives in the taiga in the summer to reproduce. The nests of this species are built in the forks of tree branches in the most inaccessible locations. Usually three eggs are laid. At an age of only four weeks, the young start to leave the nest to roost on the nearby tree branches. At the age of forty days, they make their first short flights to nearby trees. Soon afterward, the mother gives them the first lessons in hunting.

The most unusual inhabitants of the forest are the American merganser and the "four-eyed" duck. These ducks prefer to nest in the large cavities abandoned by the black woodpeckers. Their eggs and young are relatively safe from predators in these cavities. The deafening calls of geese and swans, and the piercing cries of aquatic birds give the observer some idea of the enormous number of migratory birds that fly further north to reproduce.

Mammals

The small mammals, such as the voles, shrews, and lemmings, are often difficult to observe. The red-backed voles, wood lemmings, and many species of white-toothed shrews are among the characteristic species of the Siberian taiga. They live on the forest floor and feed on the fallen seeds of conifer trees. These animals rummage through a large amount of dead needles to find the seeds.

The lemmings and voles are closely related. Their stout bodies are from 4 to 6 inches (10 to 15 cm) long. They have small eyes and ears sunken within the thick fur. During the winter, they protect themselves from the low temperatures and predators by living in a system of long tunnels and dens dug under the snow. In summer, when food is abundant, these rodents multiply rapidly. A female lemming gives birth to several litters in one season, each litter containing up to twelve offspring. The young of the first litter (and sometimes even the second) can, in turn, reproduce before the arrival of winter. In fact, the age of sexual maturity is only nineteen days, and the females give birth after only twenty days of pregnancy. Therefore, the forest floor literally teems with these young rodents.

Over several years, the populations of lemmings and voles (and other small rodents, too) can become very large or very small. This results from the combination of several factors. The most important one is the scarcity of food during years of low seed production. Conditions of over-crowding lead to more aggressive behavior and reduced matings. Another factor is the large number of rodents killed by predators attracted to the area.

The white-toothed shrews resemble the voles and lemmings. However, they belong to a different order of classification. They are classified as insectivores (insect-eaters). Unlike voles and lemmings, the shrew is character-ized by a long, sensitive nose at the end of the snout. It also has pointed teeth for chewing insects.

Two very skillful climbers live in the trees—the com-mon squirrel and its relative, the flying squirrel. The flying squirrel does not truly fly. This animal has a large flap of furry skin on each side of the body. These flaps act as a parachute while the animal leaps from one tree to another. Unlike the common squirrel, the flying squirrel is entirely nocturnal and has large protruding eyes. Its main enemies are owls, which attack at night, and humans, especially in Siberia. The flying squirrel is hunted for its soft and silky fur. In the spring, the female gives birth to two to four young, in a nest built inside a tree cavity.

The chipmunks are similar to the squirrels. The Asiatic chipmunk inhabits the Siberian taiga. It is about 5 inches (13 cm) long, with a thick 3-inch (8-cm) tail. The furry grayish red back is crossed by five brown or black stripes that run along the length of the body. The Asiatic chipmunk is also an able climber. However, it prefers to live on the ground in the piles of litter that accumulate between the roots of trees. It has ample cheek pouches in which it can carry seeds and nuts. This rodent can thus gather food supplies that weigh up to 4.5 pounds (2 kg). The Asiatic chipmunk spends the winter in a state of semihibernation.

Several different types of mammals prey on these small vegetarian mammals. Some of the predators, such as the

sable, the ermine, and the Siberian weasel, belong to the weasel family. All are characterized by a long, slender body, short legs, and a thick, soft fur. The sable is about 16 inches (40 cm) long, with a 6-inch (15-cm) tail. Its fur can vary in color from light yellow to almost black. The most frequent coloring is dark brown. The sable generally lives on the ground, hunting rodents during the day. In the winter, it takes shelter in a well-insulated den. For many years, this graceful animal has been intensively hunted and trapped for its valuable fur. Its populations have thus undergone a constant decrease in numbers. This scarcity has raised the market price for its fur.

The first laws to protect the sable were passed around 1920. After much research, the first sable ranches were established. At first, the sables were raised in captivity to repopulate the areas in which this species had disappeared. Later, these animals were raised for the commercial production of furs. Since the middle of this century, the sable has regained the population levels it had in 1600.

Both the Siberian weasel and the smaller ermine—which is about 10 inches (26 cm) long with a 4-inch (10-cm) tail—are extraordinarily swift and agile runners. Their small eyes have a very keen vision. They furiously pounce on voles and other prey that cannot flee quickly enough. Sometimes these prey include animals that are larger than the weasel and the ermine.

In the summer, the ermine has a brown fur with a white underside. In the fall, the fur changes to white and becomes considerably thicker. By the time winter sets in, the fur is completely white except for the tip of the tail, which remains black. At the beginning of the spring, the winter fur is shed and replaced by a summer coat. In mild climates, the ermine is brown in color throughout the year. The ermines that live at the northern edge of the taiga, however, have fur that remains completely white year-round. Likewise, the mountain hare, which also lives in the taiga, has a brown summer coat and a white winter coat.

Like the sable, the ermine was hunted and trapped for many centuries. Only the white fur was sought after, and the most valuable furs came from Siberia.

The dark wolverine is by far the largest and most ferocious carnivore among the species of the weasel family. Including a 12-inch (30-cm) tail, the wolverine measures about 4 feet (120 cm). It can easily be mistaken for a bear cub. The wolverine has a vast territory, which is marked

In the spring, when the snow melts, the wolverine moves too noisily to be able to hunt animals such as lynx, foxes, hares, and capercaillies. For this reason, in the summer, the wolverine eats mostly carcasses, eggs of birds that nest on the ground, lemmings, and young moose that have been isolated from the adults.

with glandular secretions and urine. During the winter, it hunts large animals such as deer, and it can run faster than its prey in the snow. The wolverine also hunts lynx, foxes, mountain hares, and capercaillies.

The lynx must cover a vast territory in order to hunt enough meat to survive, especially during the winter. This large, thick-furred cat sometimes dominates a hunting territory as large as 77 square miles (200 sq. km). In the cold taiga, it is important for a predator to use little energy while hunting. Therefore, if a pursuing lynx does not succeed in capturing a hare within a distance of about 200 yards, the lynx will give up.

The lynx makes its den in the dense forest, where from two to four young are born in May. The young develop slowly. At the age of eight months they still have their milk teeth and weak claws. At this point, they must still be nourished with small rodents and birds until they become strong enough to hunt on their own.

The largest members of many mammal and bird families are represented in the taiga. Examples are the capercaillie, which is the largest member of the grouse family, and the wolverine, the largest member of the weasel family. Finally, there is the moose, the largest member of the deer family. A

The lynx is a solitary hunter that moves silently and delicately over the snow. Its diet consists mainly of hares and deer, although it also eats small birds and rodents. The fluctuations in the populations of hares and deer have an effect on the lynx population.

large body mass actually helps to maintain body heat, particularly in the animal species that live in snowy, open areas. The same principle applies to the yaks, sheep, and mountain goats that live on the Tibetan plateau.

The impressive moose is widespread throughout the taiga. The male is about 8 feet (2.5 m) tall at the shoulder and has huge antlers. The snout has a swollen appearance and curves downward over the mouth. A short beard hangs below the throat. The female of this species is smaller and lacks antlers.

During the summer, the moose feeds on the young shoots and twigs of various trees, especially willows and poplars. Its height allows it to easily reach this vegetation. The moose spends a good deal of time in lakes and marshes. In the summer, it enters the water to escape the large, pesky swarms of mosquitoes and other insects. Like other deer, during the winter the moose lives off the body fat that has been stored up throughout the summer. However, a small amount of food is obtained from tree bark, mosses, lichens, and rare shrubs that grow in the clearings of the conifer forests.

Lake Baikal is seen on January 1. The small rivers flowing into the lake are frozen over. The lake will also be frozen by the end of January. More than three hundred rivers and mountain streams flow into Lake Baikal, which is the largest and deepest freshwater lake in the world. Two of the largest tributaries of the lake are the Selenge River, which comes down from the Mongolian steppes, and the Barguzin River, which flows from the east. Only one river, the deep Angara River, flows out of the lake. This fast-flowing river flows into the Yenisey River after a course of 1,200 miles (2,000 km). The water of Lake Baikal is clear and rich with oxygen. It is inhabited by many plant and animal species, including the notable Baikal seal, that are not found anywhere else in the world.

Lake Baikal

Lake Baikal is located in the southern part of eastern Siberia. It is perhaps the most interesting lake in the world. Its area of 12,159 sq. miles (31,500 sq. km) equals the combined areas of Belgium and the Netherlands. It is the largest and deepest freshwater lake in the world, reaching a depth of over 4,920 feet (1,500 m).

High mountains, covered with a dark taiga, surround the lake on all sides. Sheer rock cliffs face the water at several points. Another characteristic of this lake is its extraordinarily clear water. Even during the warmest period of the year, the top layer of the water stays cold.

The most peculiar characteristic of this lake, however, is the richness and variety of its animal and plant life. About 600 species of plants and more than 1,200 species of animals have been counted here. Three-fourths of these species are found only in Lake Baikal. The plants consist primarily of algae. Of these, the most exclusive and the most varied are the diatoms. Most diatoms are microscopic, single-celled algae. They often have unusual shapes and their cell walls have remarkable designs.

Numerous species of sponges, worms, mollusks (shellfish), and amphipod crustaceans (small shrimplike animals) feed on the diatoms, bacteria, and other microscopic organisms of the lake. The Baikal sponges grow on the rocks near the shore, to a depth of about 32 feet (10 m). The sponge colonies are branched like coral colonies and are about 1.5 feet (0.5 m) high. They have a greenish color, and they give the lake almost a marine appearance in some locations.

The amphipods are small animals that are flattened on the sides. They have many legs with peculiar modifications. Several pairs are adapted for swimming, some for jumping, and others for feeding. Lake Baikal is known for its populations of amphipods. More than two hundred species of this animal group live only in this lake. Several of them have brilliant green, yellow, or orange colors. Some species have long, slender bodies that are specialized for fast swimming and active movements on the water surface. The amphipods make up the main food source for the fish of the lake, and they are abundant everywhere there.

As far as anyone knows, forty-seven species of fish live in the lake. Half of them are exclusive to these waters. Gobies are the most numerous fish group. Many of them live near the shore among the rocks and the sand. Several species, however, are found in deeper water. The deep-water goby

This illustration of three Baikal seals was drawn from stuffed seals on display at the museum of limnology (study of lake and river life and phenomena) in Listvianka, Siberia. Fewer than five hundred Baikal seals survived in Lake Baikal at the beginning of this century. Their population was greatly reduced due to overhunting. Today, because of protective laws, their population is estimated at 75,000 animals.

species are found up to a depth of about 492 feet (150 m) while other gobies inhabit the open water.

The Baikal whitefish is important from an economic standpoint. This species makes up about two-thirds of the total annual fish catch of the lake. Graylings and other whitefish species are also included in this figure. At four to five years of age, the Baikal whitefish reaches a weight of from 10.5 to 16 ounces (300 to 450 grams) and a length of 12 inches (30 cm). During the winter, this fish lives in the open water, while in spring it moves close to the shore. Here it feeds on a variety of amphipods, worms, and gobies. In the fall, the adults swim upstream in the rivers to reproduce.

The largest fish in the lake is the Siberian sturgeon. It is also the most economically important fish in this lake. It reaches a length of 5 feet (1.5 m) and a weight of 253 pounds (115 kg). The golomianka fish is not an important food source, although it is interesting. It is less than 8 inches (20 cm) long and is semitransparent. It lives in the deeper parts of the lake, between depths of 492 and 2,296 feet (150 and 700 m). Unlike most species of fish, the golomianka gives birth to live young.

Another exclusive species of the lake is the Baikal seal, the most familiar animal of Lake Baikal. It is characterized by a dark gray color. This animal is at the top of the food chain of Lake Baikal. It feeds on fish, especially gobies and golomiankas. It is a small seal, measuring 5.5 feet (1.7 m) in length. At the end of the last century, due to excessive hunting, the population of Baikal seals probably numbered fewer than five thousand animals. A strict protection of the species has enabled the seal population to make a comeback to its present number of 75,000.

The most crowded breeding sites are the Ushkani islands. Here the seals gather in enormous numbers during May and June. The young are born in February or March. When the female is about to give birth, she builds a den in the ice and snow in which the newborn is kept and raised. The adult males and the younger seals remain in the water for most of winter. They breathe through holes they make in the thick layer of ice covering the water.

Considerable research has been conducted at the aquatic biology station of Lake Baikal. Based on the results, scientists believe that the smallest native organisms could have originated from the animals of an enormous saltwater lake that covered central Asia several million years ago. This lake later divided into several basins. Some of these,

The Baikal seal is the dominant predator of the huge lake from which its name derives. This animal feeds mainly on goby fish. The goby fish prey on crustaceans such as amphipods. The amphipods feed on bacteria, algae, diatoms, and other minute organisms. These small organisms constitute the plankton, which are the basis of the food chain of the lake.

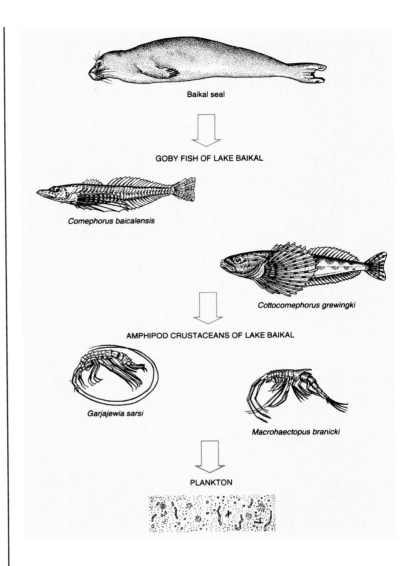

Baikal seal

↓

GOBY FISH OF LAKE BAIKAL

Comephorus baicalensis

Cottocomephorus grewingki

↓

AMPHIPOD CRUSTACEANS OF LAKE BAIKAL

Garjajewia sarsi

Macrohaectopus branicki

↓

PLANKTON

such as the Caspian Sea, were saltwater basins. Others, such as Lake Baikal, were freshwater basins. The specialized plants and animals of Lake Baikal began to evolve 25 million years ago, when the basin of the lake was created. However, the fish and the Baikal seal seem to have evolved in more recent times. The ancestors of the Baikal seal could have arrived in the lake from the Arctic Ocean, swimming along rivers. They may have crossed sections of dry land. Evidence that supports this theory is the presence of a species of tick found on the Baikal seals. This same tick is common among the arctic seals.

FROM THE RUSSIAN STEPPES TO THE URAL MOUNTAINS

A wide belt of steppe crosses the Asian continent from the western border of the Soviet Union. It extends across the Kazakh region in central Asia, as far as the Altai Mountains. These territories consist mainly of grasslands without trees. Further north, one finds a continuous belt of grasslands with trees that is almost as wide. These two regions make up the most fertile territories of Russia. Only a few isolated protected areas have not been changed for farm use. North of the tree-filled steppe and east of the Ural Mountains is a vast triangular-shaped area. This area is covered by lush forests of broadleaf trees. The mountain chain of the Urals extends for 1,200 miles (2,000 km) in a north-south direction. This chain constitutes a natural border between the plains of eastern Europe and Siberia.

The Steppes

The steppe region is characterized by a mild climate, with average temperatures of 71° to 75°F (22° to 24°C) in July. The average temperatures in January range from 29°F (-2°C) at the western edges, to -4°F (-20°C) in the eastern part. The annual rainfall for the entire region is 10 to 17 inches (250 to 450 mm). The moisture from the rainfall is much less than the amount of water lost by evaporation. Therefore, the dry periods are fairly long. Occasionally, dust storms occur. There are signs of a strong wind erosion and washing away of the soil throughout the region. The dry periods are too harsh to allow the growth of trees. The natural vegetation consists primarily of such grasses as fescue, crested hair-grass, and grasses of the *Stipa* genus. The grasses are green and luxuriant in the spring. They remain green until the beginning of summer. In the arid season at the end of the summer, they become yellow and brown.

The makeup of plant species in the grassland varies from north to south, as the climate gradually becomes drier in this direction. The northern steppes have a greater variety of plant species. The grasses are mixed with herbs and many wild flowers. These include wild tulips, irises, anemones, daisies, and sages. When the snow melts in the spring, all these plants suddenly burst into bloom and cover the steppe with red, yellow, and blue carpets. Further south, where the environment is drier, the flowers are much more scarce. Here, the vegetation is dominated by tufts of grasses of the *Stipa* genus. Herbs with deep roots that reach the lower layers of the soil are also common in this region.

Opposite page: This landscape is found in the Ural Mountains. The chain of the Urals is about 1,200 miles (2,000 km) long. It is the western limit of the Asian continent. The Urals are not extremely high in elevation. The average elevation of the crests barely reaches 3,280 feet (1,000 m). The highest peak, Narodnaya, is under 6,560 feet (2,000 m) in elevation. The Urals contain valuable mineral resources, including one of the world's largest deposits of platinum.

The soils of the steppe are called *chernozems*, which in the Russian language means "black soil." These soils are characterized by very black topsoil and abundant decomposed plant matter. On the steppe, the dense root systems of herbs decay and contribute the organic matter necessary to form the dark humus in the soil. Earthworms and other soil animals and fungi help to change the organic matter into humus. The soil bacteria contribute by releasing the nitrogen, calcium, and other elements that are important nutrients for plants.

As the steppe was gradually changed into fields for farming, the bird populations also changed. For example, the black Asiatic crow, the house sparrow, the Eurasian tree sparrow, and the common starling have appeared where they were once absent. These species prefer areas where grains are grown.

Some of the most common birds of the steppe are the great bustard and the meadow bustard. The great bustard is one of the largest flying birds in the world. It is similar to a large turkey. Its plumage is brown with black spots. Its legs are longer than a turkey's legs and its wingspan is a little over 8 feet (2.5 m). The great bustards prefer open territories

With the size of a turkey, the great bustard is one of the largest flying birds. It lives alone or in small groups in the steppe regions of central Asia. It also lives in central Europe and North America. Its nest consists of a hole dug in the ground and lined with plant stubble. The female lays two to three eggs at a time.

Larks are adaptable birds, occupying habitats both in the hills and in the plains, in sandy zones, or near cultivated fields. They live in groups for most of the year, sometimes forming huge flocks.

where they are effectively hidden by their camouflaged plumage.

Another bird of the steppe is the demoiselle crane. With a height of less than 3 feet (1 m), this bird is smaller than the other crane species. It is characterized by tufts of feathers at the sides of the head. The demoiselle is perhaps the most beautiful of all the cranes. Like the other cranes, the demoiselle crane prefers living in groups, except during the mating season. It usually lives in numerous flocks, with guards always on the lookout for possible danger.

Numerous species of larks live in this region. These include the black lark, the Siberian lark, and the skylark. These small birds are easily identified by their beautiful singing. Their plumage is mostly brown with black spots. These colors blend perfectly with the environment in which they live. The importance of such colors in hiding from predators is understandable when one considers that these birds live and nest on the ground.

Several birds of prey can be seen on the steppe. They include the steppe eagle, the imperial eagle, the pale marsh hawk, and the falcon *Falco naumanni*. The brown steppe

eagle is known for its sluggish and lazy behavior. It remains on the ground for long periods. When it finally does fly, it remains near the ground and rarely makes the effort to gain much altitude. It builds its nest on mounds of soil or stones. The eagle feeds mainly on frogs and animal carcasses.

The pale marsh hawk is smaller than the steppe eagle. It measures only about 20 inches (50 cm). The male has a glowing white plumage on the throat and breast, and bluish green wings. The female is a dark brown color. Marsh hawks typically fly over a well-defined area in search of prey. They have a showy courtship flight. When the young are hatched, the parents become extremely aggressive.

At one time, the steppes were inhabited by numerous populations of herbivores. They helped maintain the natural balance in the environment. The movement of their hooves on the ground helped to bury plant seeds. Their grazing kept the vegetation from growing excessively, and their droppings fertilized the soil. Spaces were created between the tufts of vegetation where small young plants could grow. Due to the considerable changes undergone by the steppe environment in recent centuries, many of these plant-eating mammals have become extinct. Some of the survivors are the tarpan, or wild horse (which is now extinct in the wild), and the Asiatic wild ass.

The saiga is an antelopelike animal. At one point it was on the verge of extinction. Its population has made a tre-

The steppe is inhabited by a large number of burrowing rodents. The ground in certain areas is dotted by the entrance holes of their tunnels. A variety of carnivores limits the growth of their populations. These include polecats and snakes. In the drawing, *from left to right:* whip snake, marbled polecat, Orsini's viper, black-bellied hamster, steppe lemming, mole rat, European ground squirrel, and steppe marmot.

mendous comeback in recent years, and it is now among the most numerous of the hoofed species. The saiga is a pretty animal and is the size of a goat. It has lyre-shaped horns and a large, round nose at the end of the snout. The extraordinary reproductive rate of the saiga makes up for the high number of animals killed by the severe weather. The female can reproduce when she is only seven months old. Pregnancy lasts five months. While a majority of hoofed animals give birth to only one offspring at a time, the saiga bears twins in more than half of the pregnancies.

The most numerous animals of the steppe are the burrowing rodents. They have specialized features for digging in the ground, where they spend the greater part of their time. Examples of these animals are the ground squirrels, steppe marmots, mole rats, steppe lemmings, and black-bellied hamsters. The steppe pikas are also very common, along with jerboas. Every year these small underground mammals bring thousands of tons of earth to the surface. In this way, they help maintain the soil and the vegetation.

The ground squirrels are smaller than the tree squirrels. They are reddish brown rodents characterized by stout bodies, large protruding eyes, and short tails. They live in colonies that burrow an extensive system of deep tunnels. In the areas of these colonies, the ground is dotted by a large number of entrance and exit holes. There have been known to be more than 1,200 holes in an area of 400 sq. yards (330 sq. m).

The ground squirrels are small rodents that are closely related to the squirrels. They live in underground dens across the vast plains of Asia and eastern Europe. Their diet consists of acorns, seeds, and grasses. They hibernate during the winter and reawaken in the spring at the beginning of the mating season. The females bear litters of three to eight young, which become independent by the fall. The photograph shows a common ground squirrel that has just come out of its den.

Unlike the ground squirrels, which are active during the day, the jerboas come out of their solitary dens only in the cool of the night. The jerboas look like miniature kangaroos. They have very long hind legs, short front legs, and a long tail. Their pale coat of hair blends in extremely well with the environment. The jerboas move with a succession of rapid hops. In one hop they can cover a distance of more than 3 feet (1 m). To survive the cold, the jerboas dig a "winter tunnel" that can reach a length of 10 feet (3 m).

Many predators feed on these small mammals. Among the predators are the marbled polecat, the wolf, several

birds of prey, and numerous reptiles. The reptiles include the steppe viper and the whip snake.

Insects are abundant in this region. The strong-flying species that can withstand the strong winds are especially dominant. There are also many insects that seldom fly, such as the beetles. More than five thousand species of beetles live in this environment. Other common insects are various species of locusts, grasshoppers, wasps, ants, and sawflies.

The Wooded Steppe

This region is composed of small wooded areas with gray forest soils. These areas alternate with prairie grasslands over black soils (chernozems). This entire area is characterized by cold, snowy winters and warm, relatively humid summers. The average temperature in July is 68° to 71°F (20° to 22°C). The average temperature in January ranges from 23°F (-5°C) in the eastern part to -4°F (-20°C) in the western part. The annual rainfall is higher here than in the treeless steppe. The average is 18 to 22 inches (500 to 600 mm) in the west and 11 to 15 inches (300 to 400 mm) in the east.

The wooded steppe is dominated by oak trees in the plains of eastern Europe. In western Siberia, where the climatic conditions are more severe, birch woods mixed with poplars and willows are more common. The prevailing tree species in central Siberia are birch, larch, and pine. The high fertility of the soils in the wooded steppe has caused this region to be one of the most developed in the Soviet Union. More than 70 percent of the area in the western part is intensively cultivated. The animals of this region include forest and steppe animals. The most typical forest animals are squirrels, hares, and, in certain zones, moose. The most common animals of the steppe environment are jerboas and ground squirrels.

The most frequently seen birds in the open areas are larks and hawks. Common birds include skylarks, black larks, Siberian larks, pallid harriers, lesser harriers, kestrels, and collared pratincoles. The collared pratincole also lives in the more arid steppe.

In the wooded areas of the steppe one encounters birds that also live in the more northern deciduous and mixed forests. These include the willow ptarmigan, the European cuckoo, the yellowhammer, the red-throated bunting, the carrion crow, and the golden oriole. Many species of European warblers, thrushes, and wagtails are also common.

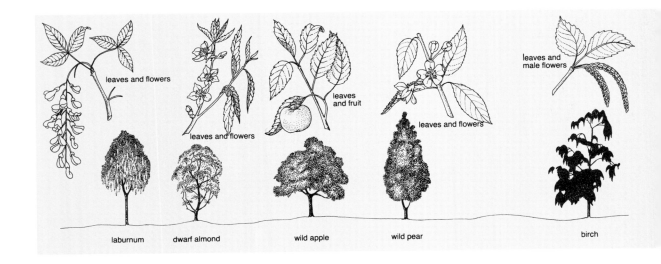

leaves and flowers

leaves and flowers

leaves and fruit

leaves and flowers

leaves and male flowers

laburnum   dwarf almond   wild apple   wild pear   birch

Above: The treeless steppe gradually changes to a zone with small woodland areas alternating with steppe prairies growing on black topsoils. The illustration shows the various trees that grow on the wooded steppe.

Right: The yellowhammer is a bunting that is widespread throughout Eurasia. It inhabits open countryside with scattered trees, cultivated fields, and marshy areas. During the warm season, it feeds primarily on insects and their larvae. In the fall, the yellowhammer feeds mostly on berries, while in the winter it eats seeds. It nests on low bushes, normally raising two broods per year.

leaves and fruit

oak

The golden oriole is a shy, insect-eating bird that usually remains well hidden in the tree foliage. It is about 8 inches long (21 cm), and the male has brilliant black and yellow colors. Its nest is built like a hammock, hanging between two branches. It is made out of grass and bark. The nest is usually built by the female, although both parents brood the eggs and raise the chicks.

Many species of diving ducks inhabit the numerous salty and freshwater lakes of the wooded steppe. The pochard and the tufted duck, which are common here, are well adapted to aquatic life. They come ashore only to sleep and to nest. They search for food by diving underwater, where they skillfully swim with the help of their webbed feet.

The surface ducks feed with their heads in the water and the tails pointing upward. In this region, they are represented by the mallard, the teal, and the shoveler. One finds the water rail and the spotted crake partially hidden among the dense shore vegetation. The spotted crake has a brownish back streaked with white, a gray breast and a yellow beak that is red at the base. It is difficult to see this bird, although it has an unmistakable shrill call. It feeds on freshwater snails, water beetles, mayflies, and mosquitoes. The spotted crane rarely flies, except when it migrates south for the winter.

The Deciduous Forest

North of the wooded steppe is a triangular-shaped area. It is bordered by the Gulf of Finland, the southern Urals, and the Carpathian Mountains. In this area, there are luxuriant forests of broadleaf trees. The region is characterized by mild summers in which the average July temperature is 66°F (19°C). The winters are long, and they have a lot of snow. The average temperature in January ranges from 20° to 23°F (-5° to -7°C). The annual rainfall averages between 22 and 26 inches (600 and 700 mm). These climatic conditions, as well as a longer growing season, produce broadleaf forests with green, paper-thin leaves.

The loss of water vapor from the leaf surface is not as critical here as in the taiga. Moderate amounts of rain fall in the summer, and there are no dry periods. Almost all the trees in these forests are deciduous. They lose their leaves at the same time, just before winter.

The bay oak is the dominant tree species of these forests. It is found in areas where the soil is deep and fertile.

ashen woodpecker

European roller

chaffinch

blue tit

hawfinch

male

Like the other oaks, it has characteristic acorns and is often long lived. Acorns are oval seeds that are protected by a cap covered with scales.

Mixed in with the oaks are various species of ashes, lime trees, maples, and elms. The ashes reach the same size as the oaks and have large compound leaves (leaves that are composed of a series of leaflets). In late spring, the leaves of the ash come out of large brownish black buds. Violet flowers emerge after the leaves. They produce clusters of winged seeds that hang from the tree throughout the following winter.

The elms are rarely found in large groups in one region. They are usually found alone, scattered here and there in the forest. The elms are also large trees, with oval leaves that are slightly toothed. They produce a great quantity of winged seeds, and every autumn they lose their leaves. When the leaves are gone, the elms have an eerie appearance, with many small twigs at the end of each branch.

In the shade, under the canopy of these large trees, is a dense undergrowth of hazelnut shrubs, climbing bittersweet, and honeysuckles. A variety of animals lives on the ground among this brush.

The birds of this temperate forest have a greater variety and number of species than any region discussed in this chapter. There are many migrating species. These include species that migrate here from the north, as well as those that winter here and nest further north. The most characteristic species of the area are the green woodpecker, a pied woodpecker, the European roller, and the tawny owl. Nightingales, the golden oriole, the chaffinch, the blue tit, the hawfinch, and many species of European warblers also inhabit this area.

The European roller is a large, stocky bird. It measures about 12 inches (30 cm) in length. Its plumage is pale blue with a light brown back, and the wings are bright blue with a black trim at the edge. It often perches in open zones, where it captures insects in flight with its large beak.

The most common mammals of the temperate forests are rodents. These include red-backed voles, field mice, and numerous species of dormice, such as the common dormouse, the tree dormouse, and the garden dormouse. The field mouse is about 3.5 inches (9 cm) long, with an equally long tail. It has a patch of reddish yellow fur under the throat and around the neck.

The large mammals of the deciduous temperate forest

Above: The yellow-throated field mouse is 3.5 to 5 inches (9 to 12 cm) long, with tail of 3 to 5 inches (8 to 13 cm). It feeds a mainly on seeds and other plant food. It sets aside stores of food for the winter.

Following pages: The European wildcat prefers forest environments. However, it also frequents the banks of rivers and mountain streams. It captures such fast prey as mice, dormice, squirrels, hares, and small birds. Occasionally, it preys on roe deer fawns. The European wildcat is nocturnal, spending the day inside a hollow tree or inside cracks between rocks.

include the wisent (European buffalo), the roe deer, the red deer, and the wild boar. There are also smaller mammal species, such as the European mink, the European wildcat, and the marten.

The Ural Mountains

The Ural region consists of a system of mountain chains extending for 1,200 miles (2,000 km) in a north to south direction. The width of this region varies from 24 miles (40 km) to more than 93 miles (150 km). The highest mountains are found to the north, where there are also several glaciers. The glaciers of this region are not extensive. The climate in the Ural region is continental. On the western side, the average temperature in January is -4°F (-20°C) in the north and 5°F (-15°C) in the south. On the eastern side,

the average January temperature ranges from -7°F to 4°F (-22° to -16°C). The average temperature in July ranges from 48° to 50°F (9° to 10°C) in the northern part, and to 66° to 68°F (19° to 20°C) in the southern part. The northern part has the most rainfall with up to 37 inches (1,000 mm), and it is also characterized by abundant snow.

The different climatic conditions and land formations result in a sequence of natural environments. These environments correspond to different latitudes. This succession, or sequence, of different environments from north to south is also evident in a vertical direction. Different elevations of the same mountain massif (mountainous mass with separate peaks) have different conditions. In the southern Urals, one finds environments of steppe and wooded steppe. Such environments are found most often on the eastern slopes. Meanwhile, the valleys near water are covered by woods of black poplars, willows, and Siberian pea trees. The steppes abound in rodents and hares. The most common birds are kestrels and common buzzards.

The forest landscapes are varied. Dark conifer forests prevail on the western slopes, with Siberian spruces and Siberian firs. In the more humid zones, at the foot of the mountain, one finds mixed forests of Siberian fir, Siberian spruce, British oak, Norway spruce, lime tree, and elm. On the eastern slopes are light conifer forests. The predominant trees in these forests are pines and larches. The forests of the northernmost zones are composed of Siberian spruce and occasionally Siberian fir and Siberian pine.

The animals of this region are more or less the same as those of neighboring areas. They consist of moose, brown bears, wolverines, lynx, and wolves. The sable is found only in the north. In the south especially, one finds badgers, polecats, and numerous reptiles and amphibians. Among the reptiles and amphibians are the European viper, the European water snake, and the viviparous (bearing live young instead of laying eggs) lizard. The most common birds are capercaillies, black grouse, mountain francolins, thick-billed nutcrackers, cuckoos, nightingales, and European redstarts.

Above the forests, one encounters the cold environments of the high elevations. These environments are inhabited by arctic foxes, rough-legged buzzards, snowy owls, and rock ptarmigans. In the summer months, one can also find herds of reindeer browsing in the pastures of the high peaks.

GUIDE TO AREAS OF NATURAL INTEREST

Japan, China, and Soviet Asia have numerous areas of great natural, interest. These areas are important for their beautiful landscapes and for the treasured species of animals and plants that live there.

In Japan, more than in any other country of the world, the national parks (twenty-seven in all) are not treated as special reserves. They are not areas set aside for the protection of particular plant or animal species, where people are forbidden to set foot. In fact, the Japanese national parks were selected mainly for the beauty of their landscapes. They are considered areas of outdoor recreation.

The protection of the natural wealth of Japan was begun many years ago. In China, this work was undertaken only about thirty years ago, and the efforts of the Chinese have been increasing. In this immense country there are presently 134 nature reserves. They extend over a total area of 45,934 sq. miles (119,000 sq. km). Many of these reserves have been set aside solely for the protection of particular animal species. For example, the Altun Nature Reserve is the largest in China, extending over 17,370 sq. miles (45,000 sq. km). It was established mainly to save the yak, the chiru, the snow leopard, and the wild ass from extinction. Other reserves have been created for the protection of the Chinese alligator and the Japanese crane. In 1985, China established the first coastal reserve in the central part of the Province of Kiangsu.

The numerous and extensive parks of Soviet Asia are part of a complex network of institutions. They were established by the Soviet Union for the conservation and management of its natural wealth. Protection is especially strict in the reserves called "Zapovedniki." These are areas of special natural, cultural, or scientific interest. No type of economic activity can be undertaken in these areas. The only human activities allowed are those attempting to restore or assure the natural balance of the territory. Today there are 138 Zapovedniki. The first was established in 1916 and is located at Barguzin, in the Asian part of the Soviet Union, on the eastern shore of Lake Baikal. Its foremost purpose was to guarantee the survival of the Baikal seal and the sable. At that time, the sable population was reduced to only about thirty animals. Perhaps these were the only surviving sables on earth. Today, this species is widespread across the region surrounding the lake. It is one of the most widely captured species of the twenty-five fur-bearing mammals that are legal to hunt or trap in the Soviet Union.

Opposite page: The Japanese macaque is one of the monkey species that is most able to withstand cold to mild climates. In recent years, extensive research of its behavior has been conducted. The Japanese macaque is present on three of the four major islands of Japan. It is absent on the island of Hokkaido. This photograph was taken in Honshu, in a reserve between Kyoto and Hiezan.

Following pages: The map shows the vast biogeographic area covered by this book. It indicates the main national parks and the most important nature reserves of the Soviet Union, China, and Japan.

FINLAND

BALTIC SEA

BARENTS SEA

KARA SEA

POLAND

▲ 1   ▲ 2

▲ 3

Yenisei River

5 ▲ ● Moscow

▲ 6

U r a l   M o u n t a i n s

S   O   V   I   E

Ob River

▲ 4

▲ 7

▲ 8

13 ▲

BLACK SEA

TURKEY

CASPIAN SEA

ARAL SEA

Baghdad ●

▲ 11

▲ 10   ▲ 12

Tehran ●

IRAQ

▲ 9

IRAN

Kabul ●

AFGHANISTAN   Islamabad ●

P l a t e a u
o f   T i b e

PAKISTAN

——— Political Boundaries

▲   1-29 Areas of
      Natural Interest

Delhi ●

NEPAL   ● Kathma

INDIA

SEA OF OKHOTSK

KURIL ISLANDS

Lena River

River

N I O N

14

Lake Baikal

15

16

17

18

19

20

HOKKAIDO

21

22

SEA OF JAPAN

Ulan Bator

26

JAPAN

Tokyo

MONGOLIA

NORTH KOREA

23

24

P'yŏngyang

Seoul

Beijing

SOUTH KOREA

SHIKOKU

Hwang Ho

25

KYUSHU

CHINA

YELLOW SEA

EAST CHINA SEA

27

PACIFIC OCEAN

Yangtze River

HUTAN

TAIWAN

28

29

Hong Kong

SOVIET UNION

Byelovezhskaya
Pusheka (1)

This reserve of 531 sq. miles (1,375 sq. km) is located about 18 miles (30 km) from Brest-Litovsk. It reaches elevations of between 492 and 557 feet (150 and 170 m) above sea level. About 289 sq. miles (749 sq. km) belong to the Soviet Union, and the remaining 242 sq. miles (627 sq. km) are part of Poland.

The majority of the park is composed of lowland forests that are flooded, especially in the fall. About 7 percent of the area is permanently flooded. In the southern part of the reserve, a chain of low hills makes up the watershed between the basins of the Niemen, Bug, and Pripet rivers. The Narev, Narevka, and Lyesna rivers flow near the boundaries of the reserve.

The vegetation is dominated by pine forests, which cover more than 50 percent of the area. Mixed forests of pine, fir, and alder are also found here. There are numerous cultivated woods of aspen, along with tracts of oaks and hornbeams. The forest areas alternate with vast marshy zones, wet meadows, and peat bogs.

This large variety of environments is inhabited by numerous animals such as the wisent, the roe deer, the badger, the fox, the wolf, and the lynx. Others are the raccoon dog, the weasel, the ermine, the polecat, the marten, and many species of dormice and squirrels. There are numerous rodents, such as field mice, harvest mice, birch mice, field mice, red-backed voles, meadow voles, and wood voles. The shrews are also abundant.

Among the birds are the red kite, Ural owl, bullfinch, the three-toed woodpecker, green woodpecker, pied woodpecker, the great reed warbler, barred warbler, and the peregrine falcon. Others are the goshawk, sparrow hawk, kestrel, honey buzzard, mountain francolin, black grouse, capercaillie, European woodcock, ruff, snipe, white stork, and black stork.

The amphibians include the common European frog the European edible frog, and the tree frog. There are common European toads, green toads, natterjack toads, spadefoot toads, fire-bellied toads, and warty newts. Among the reptiles one finds the legless slowworm lizard, the European water snake, the smoothsnake, and the European pond turtle.

Berezina (2)

This reserve of 295 sq. miles (765 sq. km) includes the upper course of the Berezina River in Belorussia. It was established for the protection and reproduction of beavers.

The forest areas are primarily composed of pines (42

percent), birches (23 percent), black alders (18 percent), and spruces (12 percent).

The numerous marshes and canals of this reserve are the preferred environments of beavers. A wide variety of animals inhabits the reserve. These include southern and northern species. Research on the ecology of beavers, otters, and many species of hoofed animals is conducted here.

Darwin (3)

This reserve is located on the Mologa-Sheksna plain near the artificial Lake Rybinsk. It was created with the aim of protecting some natural environments of the southern taiga in the European part of the Soviet Union.

The forest cover is composed mainly of pines. However, there are also forests of birches and spruces. Small stands of black alder are more rare. The forest soil is often flooded or covered by an undergrowth of mosses and blueberries. There are also peat bogs.

The reserve is inhabited by brown bears, European otters, badgers, martens, ermines, squirrels, and moose. One also finds mountain hares, capercaillies, and rock ptarmigans. Many species of aquatic and marsh birds are present, especially during the migrating seasons.

Chernozem (4)

This reserve of 20 square miles (50 sq. km) is located in the belt of wooded steppe in the European part of the Soviet Union.

Oak forests occupy 32 percent of the forest area. These woods alternate with untouched prairies, the original vegetation of the steppe. The steppe is composed of various types of grasses, such as Hungarian brome grass and grasses of the *Stipa* genus. Many flowering herbs give the steppe a very picturesque appearance. The steppe vegetation is characterized by a high plant density, which sometimes reaches 1,200 plants per square yard (1,000 per sq. m).

The reserve is inhabited by 40 species of mammals. These include moose, roe deer, wild boar, foxes, European hares, martens, stone martens, and mole rats. There are 150 species of birds, 89 of which nest in the reserve. Examples are the black kite, the nightingale, the European cuckoo, the red woodpecker, and many species of Old World warblers. Among the rarest birds are the hoopoe and the corn crake. Occasionally great bustards are seen in flight. Six species of reptiles make their home in this reserve. They include the Orsini's viper and the European fence lizard.

Oka (5)

This reserve of 23 sq. miles (60 sq. km) was created in 1953 to protect a unique natural environment in central Russia. It is the closest reserve to Moscow.

The reserve includes a transition zone between the mixed forest of broadleaf and conifer trees and the wooded steppe. In the forests one finds associations of woody and nonwoody species. These species are typical of both the northern and the southern vegetation types. Some typical plants of the steppe are also found here, such as *Stipa* grasses, fescues, and fritillarias. These plants spread northward along the valley of the Oka River. Forests of oak are found side by side with pine forests. At the eastern edge of the reserve is a natural transition zone between the forest and the steppe. By covering a distance of only 5 miles (8 km), one passes from ancient pine forests to the prairies of the steppe.

Animals of the reserve include moose, roe deer, wild boars, badgers, martens, hares, squirrels, dormice, capercaillies, mountain francolins, and black grouse. Beavers have become adapted to the zone. The European otter has spread from the reserve into the outlying areas, along the Oha River.

Pechora-Ilych (6)

This reserve is located on the western slopes and the piedmont zone (base of a mountain) of the northern Urals. It was established in 1930 to protect the natural environment of the northeastern part of European Russia, especially the habitat of the sable. The area is subject to abundant snow precipitation. In January, the average temperature is 0°F (-18°C). The average summer temperature is between 54° and 59°F (12° and 15°C).

The reserve includes three different natural regions. One is the plain of the Pechora River, which is covered by pine forests. The second is the piedmont zone of the Urals, with spruce forests, fir forests, and mixed forests of fir, spruce, and cedar. The third is the mountain zone of the Urals, with well-defined bands of vegetation at different elevations.

The most common animals include moose, brown bears, wolves, European otters, willow ptarmigans, nutcrackers, crossbills, Siberian jays, and wall lizards. The sable and the marten occupy the same environments. They have been known to crossbreed occasionally. Beavers have recolonized the area (the wild population of this species was wiped out at the beginning of the 1800s). The upper course of the Pechora River is one of the main breeding

Ilmen (7)

Bashkir (8)

Ramit (9)

Chatkal (10)

areas of salmon. Other fish present are graylings, whitefish, and taimens *(Hucho taimen).*

This reserve is located on the eastern side of the southern Urals, in the region of Cheliabinsk Oblast, northeast of the city of Miass. It includes a 34-mile (55-km) section of the Ilmen mountains, the Kosaia Gora chain, and numerous lakes. The area was established as a reserve in 1953 to protect the rock formations and their unusual mineral compositions.

This reserve of 278 sq. miles (720 sq. km) is located in the central part of the southern Urals and in the basin of the Belaya River. It was established in 1930 for the conservation and the study of wooded steppe environments and the typical forests of these zones.

Forests of pine, larch, and birch are present along the chains of the southern Urals, the Uraltans, and Iuzhnyi Krala. The most common animals of the region are moose, roe deer, brown bears, lynx, martens, Siberian weasels, capercaillies, and mountain francolins. In the basin of the Belaya River, one finds mixed forests or broadleaf trees. Graylings, salmon, and trout live in the rivers. The famous cave of Kapova is located in the park.

This reserve is located on the southern slopes of the Gissar Mountains. It was created to protect the forest, which is mainly composed of fruit trees, walnut trees, and thickets of junipers. The vegetation includes maples, cherries, plums, wild apples, almonds, honeysuckles, barberries, pistachios, European walnuts, junipers, birches, and poplars.

The more common animals are porcupines, long-tailed marmots, tree dormice, stone martens, and brown bears. Other common animals include Himalayan snow grouse, alpine choughs, Eurasian dippers, Asiatic dippers, hawfinches, Indian paradise flycatchers, and ibis bills.

This reserve is located on the western ridge of the Chatkal mountain range, about 42 miles (70 km) from Tashkent. It was established in 1947 to protect the natural environments of the western Tien Shan Mountains.

Steppe environments are represented in the reserve, along with alpine meadows and a zone of bushy and shrubby vegetation. This last zone has junipers, wild pears and apples, haws, mountain ashes and wild cherries.

The mammals of the reserve include the tur (wild goat), the roe deer, the wild boar, the Siberian marmot, the porcupine, and the brown bear. Others are the wolf, the fox, the badger, the marten, the ermine, and the weasel. The snow leopard is an occasional inhabitant. The most frequent bird species are the Himalayan snow grouse, the willow ptarmigan, the griffon vulture, the black vulture, the bearded vulture, the Egyptian vulture, and the Himalayan thrush.

Asu-Dzhabagli (11)

This reserve is found at an elevation of 6,560 feet (2,000 m) and is composed of hilly zones, plateaus, and numerous mountain peaks. The peaks belong to the Tallas-Ala-Tau mountain range, which forms a stupendous panorama for more than 150 miles (240 km). Its peaks are covered by snow year-round. The northern sides of this range slope gradually, while the southern slopes drop abruptly. From a geological standpoint, these mountains are relatively young. The upper ends of the valleys have a typical glacial structure, with steep hollows and U-shaped erosion. At the foot of the hills, the valleys have deep, narrow gorges.

There are no true forests in the reserve, only thickets of juniper cover the slopes here and there. On the prairie, one finds juniper thickets mixed with honeysuckles, fire thorn shrubs, barberries, bellflowers, and wild roses.

The zone at the foot of the mountains is inhabited by typical animals of the Asian steppe. These include jerboas, Asiatic polecats, hedgehogs, foxes, and skylarks. The steep slopes are inhabited by foxes, badgers, lynx, weasels, stone martens, Siberian wild goats, argalis, snow leopards, wolves, and red deer. Higher in elevation, in the subalpine zone, one finds marmots and brown bears.

The birds that nest primarily on the steepest mountain slopes include whitethroats, flycatchers, Oriental doves, gray-collared buntings, and redheaded buntings. Common birds of the alpine meadows include partridges, black-throated wheatears, and quails. On the cliffs and crags one finds snow finches, rock nuthatches, house martins, swifts, red-tailed rock thrushes, and blue rock thrushes. The Eurasian dipper, the Asiatic dipper, the penduline tit, the golden oriole, and the Indian paradise flycatcher live in humid environments close to the streams. Among the rocks, above the limit of the permanent snow, one finds the Himalayan snow grouse, the snow finch, the rock pipet, the alpine accentor, the horned lark, the Buchanan's bunting, the wall creeper, and Brandt's finch.

Opposite page: A Russian horse-drawn sled, or troika, stops in a birch forest during the Siberian winter. These sleds are still used in the beautiful parks of the Soviet Union, and especially in Siberia.

111

Sary-Chelek (12)

This reserve is located on the crest of the Chatkal mountains in the Tien-Shan Mountains. It was established for the preservation of the forest of walnut and fruit trees. The elevations range from 3,936 feet (1,200 m) to 13,930 feet (4,247 m) of elevation.

More than one thousand species of plants grow within the reserve. Up to an elevation of 6,888 feet (2,100 m), the vegetation is dominated by forests of European walnut and wild apple. Higher up, in the subalpine zone, firs and spruces prevail. The spruces are found up to an elevation of 9,840 feet (3,000 m). At higher elevations, the vegetation consists of alpine meadows.

The animals include wild boars, roe deer, mountain goats, argalis, brown bears, porcupines, long-tailed marmots, snow grouse, chukar partridges, penduline tits, and Eurasian dippers. There are many aquatic birds in the lakes, especially in the summer and fall.

Altai (13)

This reserve of 3,373 sq. miles (8,740 sq. km) is one of the largest in the Soviet Union. It is located in the northeastern part of the Altai Mountains. The southern part of the reserve includes alpine environments. Here, the tree limit is at an elevation of between 5,905 and 6,235 feet (1,800 and 1,900 m).

From north to south, one finds a succession of fir forests, then mixed forests of fir and cedar, then pure stands of cedar, then mixed forests of cedar and larch, and finally pure stands (groups of only one species) of larch.

Lake Teletskoye is located in the center of the reserve. It is almost 50 miles (80 km) long and just under 4 miles (6 km) wide. There are numerous mineral springs throughout the reserve. Many mammals go to these springs to drink and to lick salt.

The reserve is inhabited by sixty species of mammals, three hundred bird species, and ten species of amphibians and reptiles. The animals include argalis, Mongolian gazelles, moose, musk deer, Siberian wild goats, and brown bears. There are also squirrels, longtailed ground squirrels, Asiatic chipmunks, northern pikas, Altai pikas, snow leopards, Altai grouse, willow ptarmigans, and demoiselle cranes.

Barguzinsky (14)

This reserve of 968 sq. miles (2,510 sq. km) is located on the eastern edge of Lake Baikal, about 656 feet (200 m) above sea level. Besides the lake, it includes a large part of the Barguzinsky mountain range.

Half of the reserve is located in an alpine zone, where there are hot springs surrounded by willows and birches. Next to the rivers are wet meadows and peat bogs with larches and cranberry trees. The plants of the reserve include many species of anemone, columbine, geranium, mountain avens, spiraea, cinquefoil, and *Thelycrania*. There are also honeysuckles, wild roses, red currants, black currants, larches and pines. From January to May, the lake is completely frozen over, and the temperatures range from -4°F (-20°C) in the winter to 50°F (10°C) in the summer. In the mountains, it snows throughout the year except for the month of July. In the fall, strong winds blow at more than 87 miles (140 km) per hour and create fantastic gorges in the ice along the shores of the lake.

The mammals of the reserve include sables, ermines, wolverines, European otters, brown bears, reindeer, moose, Siberian red deer, and musk deer. Others are Asiatic chipmunks, Kamchatka marmots, northern pikas, red-backed voles, and wood lemmings. The birds include brown-capped chickadees, European nuthatches, willow warblers, red crossbills, and white-winged crossbills. Thick-billed nutcrackers, three-toed woodpeckers, jays, white wagtails, gray wagtails, and yellow wagtails also inhabit the reserve. In addition, there are sandpipers, red-throated buntings, collared buntings, swifts, geese, swans, white-tailed eagles, capercaillies, mountain francolins, willow ptarmigans, rock ptarmigans, Japanese quail, Siberian jays, and pine grosbeaks.

Khekhtsir (15)

This reserve of 172 sq. miles (447 sq. km) is located in the southwestern part of the Khekhtsir mountain range, south of the city of Khabarovsk, where the Ussuri and Amur rivers flow together.

The vegetation is composed of typical plants of the southern Ussuri region. The most common tree species are the Korean pine, the Dahurian larch, the Amur cork tree, the Japanese elm, the yellow birch, and various species of spruce, fir, ash, oak, and walnut.

The animals include red deer, roe deer, musk deer, wild boars, sables, Siberian weasels, yellow-throated martens, otters, and foxes.

Others are raccoon dogs, lynx, Asiatic black bears, brown bears, badgers, squirrels, Manchurian hares, mountain francolins, black grouse, pheasants, mandarin ducks, and Chinese softshell turtles.

Sikhote-Alinski (16)

This reserve of 1,212 sq. miles (3,140 sq. km) is located in the extreme southeastern part of the Soviet Union. It includes a coastal strip of about 30 miles (48 km) along the Sea of Japan. The territory is mostly mountainous, with a central watershed. The watershed divides the southwestern part of the reserve from the northeastern part. The three main rivers (Sankhobe, Belimbo, and Iodzike) flow into the Ussuri River. In turn, the Ussuri River flows into the sea by way of the Amur River. There are many waterfalls. The best season to visit is fall.

Notable animals of this reserve are musk deer, sika deer, roe deer, gorals (Himalayan chamois), wild boars, lynx, and Siberian tigers. Others are leopard cats, Asiatic black bears, raccoon dogs, Siberian weasels, and yellow-throated martens. There are also northern pikas, white-backed woodpeckers, ashen woodpeckers, three-toed woodpeckers, hawfinches, white-tailed eagles, ospreys, long-eared owls, and gray-faced buzzards.

JAPAN

Rishiri-Rebun-Sarobetsu (17)

This national park is located on the northwestern edge of Hokkaido. It was established in 1974 as the twenty-seventh park in Japan. The park includes the plain of Sarobetsu and the islands of Rishiri and Rebun. The island of Rishiri, which is noted for its alpine plants, is 12 miles (20 km) from Hokkaido. It is dominated by the spectacular volcano of Mount Rishiri, with an elevation of 5,635 feet (1,718 m). The island of Rebun is known as the "island of flowers," since it also has many alpine plants. The plain of Sarobetsu is the most extensive wetland area of Japan, consisting of a vast peat bog located between two lakes.

Shiretoko (18)

This national park extends for 40 miles (65 km) along the eastern edge of Hokkaido, which faces the Sea of Okhotsk. It is known for its volcanoes, primary forests, and reefs on which numerous marine birds nest.

Akan (19)

This national park of 337 sq. miles (875 sq. km) is located in the eastern region of Hokkaido. It is well known for its magnificent, peaceful scenery. It is also famous for its beautiful lakes, mountains, and volcanoes. Several of the volcanoes, such as O-Akan, Me-Akan, and Io, give off plumes of smoke. Three lakes are particularly interesting. Lake Mashu is famous for its beautiful location and for its unusually clear, dark-blue water. The other two lakes are both large volcanic craters (calderas). Lake Kutcharo is nestled among a splendid ring of mountains. Lake Akan has four islands and a virgin forest that has yet to be fully explored. From the Bihoro pass, the Sempoku pass, and the Sokodai plateau, one can enjoy a stupendous view.

Among the trees, one finds bushes of rhododendrons and azaleas, as well as rare alpine plants. Birches and maples are found in the forests. A large part of the park is composed of a primary forest of conifers. The most famous plant of the park is an aquatic species known as "marimo."

There are numerous mammals in the park. These include brown bears, sables, ermines, squirrels, raccoon dogs, and sika deer. During the summer, white-tailed eagles, swifts, tits, dippers, Japanese warblers, and buntings can be observed near Lake Akan. Mandarin ducks, mountain francolins, collared buntings, and Gray's grasshopper warblers nest on the east side of the park, in the Teshikaga region.

Daisetsuzan (20)

This national park is the largest in Japan, located in the center of Hokkaido. It includes several volcanoes, such as Mount Tomuraushi at 7,024 feet (2,141 m), Mount Asahi at 7,513 feet (2,290 m), and Mount Tokachi at 6,814 feet (2,077 m).

The slopes are covered with extensive forests of spruces and firs. The rivers have formed picturesque canyons and gorges in their upper courses. There is a rich and varied alpine plant community at high elevations.

The zone at the foot of the mountains is inhabited by sables, squirrels, and raccoon dogs. At higher elevations, one finds brown bears, northern pikas, Asiatic chipmunks, and foxes.

Towada-Hachimantai (21)

This national park is located at the northern extremity of Honshu. It is divided into two zones. The northern part includes the region around Lake Towada. The southern part is composed of the Hachimantai plateau, and mounts Iwate, Nyuto, and Koma. The natural wealth of these regions is still untouched. There are splendid forests, crystalline lakes, and volcanic cones.

The Oirase valley extends along the river by the same name. The Oirase River flows out of Lake Towada. The park is noteworthy for its beautiful beech forests.

On the river and in the surrounding woods, one can observe Asiatic dippers, reddish kingfishers, European warblers, magpies, tits, and flycatchers.

Mount Fuji is the highest mountain in Japan, with an elevation of 12,385 feet (3,776 m). Its name means ''fire'' in the Ainu language. Mount Fuji is a volcano. Its last recorded eruption occurred in 1707. After the eruption, a 5.5-inch (15-cm) layer of ash settled over the city of Tokyo. Mount Fuji is considered a sacred mountain by the Japanese. It has been the subject of many poems and songs.

Rikuchu-Kaigan (22)

This national park extends for 111 miles (180 km) along the eastern coast of the northern end of Honshu. The landscape is varied by reefs, small bays, and inlets. The vegetation includes numerous rhododendrons. Many species of gulls and storm petrels nest here.

Chubu-Sangaku (23)

This national park of 288 sq. miles (635 sq. km) is located in the central part of Honshu. It includes the central and northern zones of a mountainous region called the "Japanese Alps." The Hida mountains are included in the park. The highest peaks in Japan, next to Mount Fujiyama, are found in this area, with elevations over 9,840 feet (3,000 m). The Japanese Alps resemble the European Alps both in landscape and in the abundance of snow they receive during the winter. The jagged peaks and snowy valleys have a truly spectacular appearance. Plateaus of lava rock and deep valleys branch off the main mountain range. The mountain slopes are covered by primary forests of conifers and broadleaf trees.

These mountains are inhabited by Japanese macaques, Formosa serows, Asiatic black bears, rock ptarmigans, and many species of alpine butterflies, as well as other animals.

Fuji-Hakone-Izu (24)

This national park of 472 sq. miles (1,223 sq. km) includes four distinct zones. They are Mount Fuji, Mount Hakone, the peninsula of Izu, and the seven islands of Izu. The landscape ranges from mountains to forests to coasts. Each zone has its own particular charm. Mount Fuji has long been considered a sacred mountain, and this part of the park is probably the most visited area of Japan. There are five artificial lakes at the base of the mountain in which tourists can fish, swim, or go boating. The main attractions in the area of Mount Fuji are the uneven shores of Lake Kawaguchi, the view of the "sea of trees" from atop Koyodai (the hill of maples), and the deep blue water of Lake Motosu. Mount Hakone, which is located between Fuji and the peninsula of Izu, is also a volcanic massif. It has fifteen hot springs, seven mineral springs, splendid forests, hills, mountains, mountain streams, a lake, and beautiful beaches.

The mammals of the park include sika deer, wild boars, Japanese macaques, and Japanese dormice. Many birds inhabit the area, including more than one hundred species of perching birds. The highest peaks are inhabited by eagles, Soemmering pheasants, and many species of woodpeckers, buntings, and tits.

Aso (25)

This national park is located in the center of the island of Kyushu. Its territory is characterized by contrasting landscapes. Green meadows and dense forests alternate with blackish brown lava deserts and mountains with strange shapes. There are two volcanic massifs, Mount Aso and Mount Kuju. The crater of Mount Aso has a diameter of from 11 to 15 miles (18 to 24 km). It is one of the largest in the world and contains five volcanic cones, one of which is still active. The plateau of Mount Kuju is covered in summer by large patches of red azaleas. There are many hot springs both within and outside the park, including Beppu and Chojabaru.

South of the park is the "crane paradise" of Arasaki, a small village near Kagoshima. From November to March, the area is invaded by white-headed cranes.

CHINA

Changbai (26)

This nature reserve is rich in species and has beautiful surroundings. The Changbai Mountains cover an area of 3,000 sq. miles (8,000 sq. km).

More than eighty species of economically important trees grow in the region. These include the Korean pine, the Dahurian larch, spruce, and Chinese ash. More than three hundred species of medicinal plants, such as ginseng, milk vetch, *Gastrodia elata*, and mezereum can be found in this park. There are two hundred species of wildflowers.

The forests covering the Changbai Mountains are inhabited by more than fifty species of mammals and more than two hundred species of birds. Furthermore, there are more than three hundred species of reptiles and fish. About a dozen animal species are rare. The Siberian tiger, the sika deer, the sable, and the lynx have been placed under protection by the Chinese authorities.

Wolong (27)

This nature reserve is located 60 miles (100 km) northeast of Chengdu, which is the capital of the Province of Szechwan. It covers an area of 500 acres (2 sq. km), between elevations of 16,400 and 20,500 feet (5,000 and 6,250 m).

A succession of different vegetation zones is found at various elevations. Starting at the bottom, there is an evergreen forest zone. This is followed by a zone of deciduous broadleaf forest, a zone of mixed forest of conifers, and broadleaf trees, a zone of conifer forests, and finally, a zone of subalpine thickets and meadows. The most common trees are the camphor tree, the Chinese hemlock, and the Chinese larch.

More than 50 percent of the animal species found in the reserve are protected by law. These animals include the giant panda, the lesser panda, the Assam macaque, the takin, and the musk deer.

This nature reserve is located northeast of the city of Zhaoqing, in the Province of Guangdong. It is near the tropic of Cancer.

The area of the Dinghu Mountains is characterized by evergreen tropical forests and monsoonal forests of broad-leaf trees. Some of these trees are more than four hundred years old. Many different types of plants grow in the protected zone. The seed-bearing plants alone number more than two thousand species. The forests are inhabited by more than one hundred species of birds, thirty species of mammals, and more than twenty species of reptiles.

The Dinghu Reserve is also a tourist area. It is notable for its deep valleys, numerous springs, and spectacular waterfalls. The reserve has become an ideal base for scientific research and education. It attracts scientists from all over the world.

HONG KONG

Because of its geographic location, in Hong Kong one can see birds that are impossible or difficult to see elsewhere. The marshes of Mai Po, at the western border with China, are good for this activity during any season of the year. Here, one can see the wary Asiatic dowitcher, the Nordmann's sandpiper, and the spoon-billed sandpiper. The nesting locations of the herons and egrets are a major attraction during the mating season. More than 350 bird species can gather in the area at one time. Among them is the rare Chinese egret.

Forest birds can be seen by visiting the state forest of Tai Po Kau. It can be reached by train from Kowloon. Other suitable locations for observing forest birds are the basin of the Jubilee (east of Tsuen Wan) and the area surrounding the village of Shek Kong.

Preceding pages: Pictured is a forest in the nature reserve of Wolong in China. This is the natural habitat of the giant panda.

GLOSSARY

adaptation change or adjustment by which a species or individual improves its condition in relationship to its environment.

amphibian any of a class of vertebrates that usually begins life in the water as a tadpole with gills and later develops lungs.

biogeography the branch of biology that deals with the geographical distribution of plants and animals.

bog wet, spongy ground; a small marsh or swamp.

botanist a plant specialist. Botanists study the science of plants, which deals with the life, structure, growth, classification, etc., of a plant or plant group.

camouflage a disguise or concealment of any kind. The silver-gray color, black spots, and rosettes of the snow leopard provide it with a natural camouflage.

carnivore a meat-eating organism such as a predatory mammal, a bird of prey, or an insectivorous plant.

conifers cone-bearing trees and shrubs, most of which are evergreens.

conservation the controlled use and systematic protection of natural resources.

continent one of the principal land masses of the earth. Africa, Antarctic, Asia, Europe, North America, South America, and Australia are regarded as continents.

crustacean any of a class of hard-shelled, segmented organisms that usually live in the water and breathe through gills.

deciduous forests forests having trees that shed their leaves at a specific season or stage of growth.

diatom any of a number of microscopic algae, one-celled or in colonies, which are a source of food for all kinds of marine life.

ecology the relationship between organisms and their environment.

environment the circumstances or conditions of a plant or animal's surroundings.

erosion natural processes such as weathering, abrasion, and corrosion, by which material is removed from the earth's surface.

evolution a gradual process in which something changes into a different and usually more complex or better form.

extinction the process of destroying or extinguishing. Many species of plant and animal life face extinction either because of natural changes in the environment or those caused by carelessness.

genus a classification of plants or animals with common distinguishing characteristics.

geology the science dealing with the physical structure and history of the earth.

gorge a deep, narrow pass between steep heights.

habitat the area or type of environment in which a person or other organism normally exists.

herbivore an animal that eats plants. Deer, antelope, and elephants are herbivores.

hibernate to spend the winter in a dormant state.

insectivore an animal that eats insects.

invertebrate lacking a backbone or spinal column.

larva the early, immature form of any animal that changes structurally when it becomes an adult. This process of change is called metamorphosis.

latitude the angular distance, measured in degrees, north or south from the equator.

marsh an area of low-lying flatland, such as a swamp or bog. The marsh is a type of borderland between dry ground and water.

migrate to move from one region to another with the change in seasons. Many animals have steady migration patterns.

mollusk an invertebrate animal characterized by a soft, usually unsegmented body, often enclosed in a shell, and having gills and a foot. Oysters, clams, and snails are mollusks.

naturalist a person who studies nature, especially by direct observation of animals and plants.

nocturnal referring to animals that are active at night.

omnivore an animal that eats both plants and other animals.

organism any individual animal or plant having diverse organs and parts that function as a whole to maintain life and its activities.

peninsula a land area almost entirely surrounded by water and connected to the mainland by a narrow strip of earth called an isthmus.

photosynthesis the process by which chlorophyll-containing cells in green plants convert sunlight into chemical energy and change inorganic compounds into organic compounds.

plankton microscopic plant and animal organisms which float or drift in the ocean or in bodies of fresh water.

plateau an elevated and more or less level expanse of land.

predator an animal that lives by preying on others. Predators kill other animals for food.

prey an animal hunted or killed for food by another.

refuge shelter or protection from danger or difficulty; a place of safety.

reptile a cold-blooded vertebrate having lungs, a bony skeleton, and a body covered with scales or horny plates. Snakes and lizards are examples of reptiles.

shrub a low, woody plant with several permanent stems instead of a single trunk; a bush.

species a distinct kind, sort, variety, or class. Plant and animal species have a high degree of similarity and can generally interbreed only among themselves.

steppe a large plain having few trees. Many of the steppes in Europe and Asia have been cultivated and planted with grain crops.

symbiosis the living together of two kinds of organisms, especially where such an association provides benefits or advantages for both. Algae and fungi in symbiosis form lichens.

temperate a climate which is neither very cold nor very hot, but rather moderate.

tundra a treeless area between the icecap and the tree line of arctic regions, having a permanently frozen subsoil.

vertebrate having a backbone or spinal column. Fish, amphibians, reptiles, birds, and mammals are primarily vertebrates, having a segmented body or cartilaginous spinal column.

viviparous bearing or bringing forth living young instead of laying eggs. There are several species of viviparous lizards in northern Asia.

INDEX

CREDITS

MAPS AND DRAWINGS. G. Vaccaro, Cologna Veneta (Verona, Italy). **PHOTOGRAPHS. A. Borroni,** Milan: 34, 88; G. Mairani 46, 54-55. **Overseas,** Milan: A. Calegari, 100-101; Explorer Carde 110; C. Galasso 91; E. Httenmoser 74; Jacana 80-81; Jacana/C. Baranger 90; Jacana/Gohier 44-45; Jacana/J.M. Labat 40-41, 83; Jacana/B. Mallet 42; Jacana/A. Rainon 82; J.P. Nacivet 30, 32-33, 116-117; NHPA/J.B. Blossom 12; NHPA/M. Danegger 72-73; NHPA/N. Dennis 62; NHPA/M. Leach 71; NHPA/M. Ranjit 25; NHPA/P. Scott 38-39; NHPA/J. Shaw 69; NHPA/R. Tidman 43; Oxford Scientific Films/M.M. Boyd 26-27; Oxford Scientific Films/J.A.L. Cooke 66; Oxford Scientific Films/J. Paling 21; Oxford Scientific Films/Press-Tige Pictures 99; Oxford Scientific Films/D.J. Saunders 58, 96-97; S. Palombi 50. **Panda Photo,** Rome: H. Ausloos cover, 53; A. Bardi 94-95, A. Boano 29; P. Harris 16-17; W. Lapinsky 77; WWF International/P. Dugan 14-15; WWF International/G.B. Schaller 11, 28, 120-121; WWF International/A. Taylor 22-23. **D. Pellegrini,** Milan: 48-49, 60-61, 63. **L. Pellegrini,** Milan: 6-7, 68, 84-85, 102. **F. Speranza,** Milan: 8.